Jeopardy! champion and *New York Times* bestselling author

KEN JENNINGS'
JUNIOR GENIUS GUIDES

MAPS AND GEOGRAPHY

BY **KEN JENNINGS**

ILLUSTRATED BY **MIKE LOWERY**

SEMPER QUAERENS

LITTLE SIMON
New York London Toronto Sydney New Delhi

THE OFFICIAL
JUNIOR GENIUS CIPHER

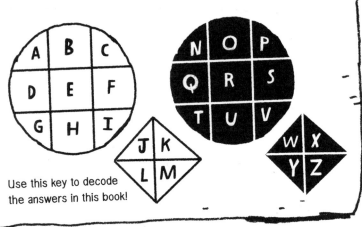

Use this key to decode
the answers in this book!

LITTLE SIMON

An imprint of Simon & Schuster Children's Publishing Division

1230 Avenue of the Americas, New York, New York 10020

Text Copyright © 2014 by Ken Jennings

Illustrations copyright © 2014 by Simon & Schuster, Inc.

All rights reserved, including the right of reproduction in whole or in part in any form.

LITTLE SIMON is a registered trademark of Simon & Schuster, Inc., and associated colophon is a

trademark of Simon & Schuster, Inc. For information about special discounts for bulk purchases,

please contact Simon & Schuster Special Sales at 1-866-506-1949 or

business@simonandschuster.com. The Simon & Schuster Speakers Bureau can bring authors to

your live event. For more information or to book an event contact the Simon & Schuster Speakers

Bureau at 1-866-248-3049 or visit our website at www.simonspeakers.com.

Manufactured in Thailand 1220 SCP

4 6 8 10 9 7 5 3

Library of Congress Cataloging-in-Publication Data

Jennings, Ken, 1974–

Maps and geography / by Ken Jennings ; illustrated by Mike Lowery. — First Edition.

pages cm. — (Ken Jennings' Junior Genius Guides)

Includes bibliographical references and index.

ISBN 978-1-4424-9848-8 (hardcover : alk. paper) — ISBN 978-1-4424-7328-7 (pbk : alk. paper)

— ISBN 978-1-4424-7329-4 (ebook) 1. Geography—Juvenile literature. 2. Maps—Juvenile

literature. I. Lowery, Mike, 1980- illustrator. II. Title.

G133.J47 2014

910—dc23

2012050862

CONTENTS

INTRODUCTION

All right, class, that's the bell. Everyone please find your seats and quiet down.

I'm Professor Jennings, and I'll be teaching today's class on maps and geography. You could probably tell I'm the teacher because I'm a lot taller than you, and I have a big desk with a nameplate that says PROFESSOR JENNINGS. Also I'm wearing a graduation hat and gown and holding a globe and I have a huge head crammed full of knowledge. Junior Geniuses: I'm here to share some of that knowledge with you.

But let me remind you that being a Junior Genius has nothing to do with the size of your noggin or the thickness of your glasses or even the grades on your report card. It's a state of mind. Junior Geniuses are interested in the world around them and excited to learn all they can about it—especially the cool, weird stuff. As the Junior Genius motto reminds us: *Semper quaerens.* That's Latin for "Always curious."

Please rise, put your right index finger to your temple, and face this drawing of Albert Einstein. We will now say the Junior Genius Pledge.

**With all my fellow Junior Geniuses,
I solemnly pledge to quest after questions,
to angle for answers, to seek out, and
to soak up. I will hunger and thirst for
knowledge my whole life through, and I
dedicate my discoveries to all humankind,
with trivia not for just us but for all.**

Very good. You may be seated!

FIRST PERIOD

The Earth from Space

"Geography" comes from the Greek word for "description of the Earth." "Geo-" means "Earth," like in "geology." The "-graphy" part means "to write," like in "graphic" or "biography." So geographers study and describe the Earth.

This is the Earth. It is our home, unless any of you are aliens who have secretly invaded our planet for your own purposes. If so, please see me after class.

You might have heard or read that Columbus proved the Earth was round in 1492, when he sailed from Spain to the Caribbean. This

is not even close to true! By Columbus's time, scientists had known the Earth was round for almost two thousand years.

The Shape the World Is In

The earliest Greek thinkers disagreed about the shape of the Earth. Thales thought it was a round, flat disk floating in water, like a pancake that's fallen overboard at sea.

Anaximander thought the Earth was a cylinder, while Anaximenes (no relation) believed it was a flat rectangle floating on compressed air.

But by 500 BC or so, most people agreed with the philosophers Pythagoras and Aristotle: The Earth was round, like a ball. There was good evidence for this.

If you really want to celebrate the discovery of round Earth, don't celebrate Columbus Day on October 12—celebrate Eratosthenes ("air-uh-TOSS-thuh-neez") Day on June 21! Eratosthenes was the Greek who invented the word "geography" and a very smart guy—in fact, he was the head librarian at the ancient world's largest library, in Alexandria. Around 240 BC, Eratosthenes devised a very clever experiment to measure the Earth. In late June, on the longest day of the year, he had two sticks placed straight in the ground in two different cities, five hundred miles apart, and measured their shadows. The shadows were different lengths, which meant the sticks weren't parallel—the Earth was round after all!

What's more, Eratosthenes could use the length of the shadow to calculate the size of the entire Earth, without ever leaving Egypt. His measurement was about 24,600 miles, and today we know that the Earth actually measures 24,902 miles around at the equator. Eratosthenes was off by just a few hundred miles!

The Accidental Tourist

Columbus, however, didn't get the memo. For his 1492 voyage, he relied on maps made by Egyptian scientist Ptolemy (the *P* is silent, luckily, or his name would be a pterrible ptongue ptwister). Ptolemy's math led him to believe that Europe and Asia were quite a bit wider than they actually are, so Columbus thought he could circle the Earth in just 16,000 miles! The world's best navigators at the time were the Portuguese, and they knew this was crazy talk. Their own guess was close to Eratosthenes's: about 26,000 miles. Columbus set off anyway, sure that he could get all the way to China and India in a matter of weeks. Luckily, there was a big

unknown continent in the way (Spoilers! It was *North America*!) or he would have been lost at sea forever. India was four times farther away than he thought, and he would have run out of supplies months before arriving.

Doing Their Level Best

Despite all the geographical evidence, there are people who still believe that the Earth is flat. The largest organization for these unscientific souls is the Flat Earth Society, founded by a British sign painter in 1956, the year before the space age began.

The Earth proposed by this group is a big, flat disk like Thales suggested, with the North Pole in the center. Antarctica is a big wall of ice around the edge, which luckily keeps the oceans from leaking off!

The society's membership peaked at about two thousand in the 1970s, but today it's down to a few hundred true believers. Of course, it's a lot harder to believe in a flat Earth now that spaceships and satellites are orbiting the Earth and sending back pictures all the time. During the 1950s, the society's founder was given one of the first photos of a round Earth taken from space. "It is easy to see how such a picture could fool the untrained eye," he calmly replied.

Let's Not Wait; It's a Really Long Line

The grid of north–south and east–west lines that you see on maps is used to mark latitude and longitude. (IMPORTANT NOTE: These lines are imaginary! You will not see them by looking out the window of an airplane!) Latitude is a measurement of how far north or south you are, while longitude measures east and west.

Official Junior Genius Way to Remember Which Is Which

"Latitude" lines go from side to side, like the rungs of a "ladder." "Longitude" lines travel from the North to South Poles—a really "long" way.

If you were to stand at one of the poles, it would take the Earth's rotation a full day to turn you in a circle—in other words, you'd be moving *veeeeery* slowly. But at the equator, the surface of the Earth rotates a *lot* faster. Standing "still" at the equator, you're actually moving at 1,070 miles per hour, faster than the speed of sound!

Math Homework

If you have an atlas (or GPS device) and a calculator with a cosine key, you can find out how fast you're spinning right now! Find your latitude in degrees, enter it into your calculator, and hit the COS button. Then multiply this answer by 1,070 miles per hour. Presto! That speed is your current velocity! Wow, you're getting a pretty good workout.

Pop Quiz!

What country's name actually means "equator" in its native language?

□◁◖◁◖◕■

Do You Come From a Land Down Under?

South of the equator is the Southern Hemisphere. Of course, no one in the Southern Hemisphere ever "falls off" the Earth—gravity keeps Australians and South Africans and Argentines firmly on the ground, just as it does for Americans and Europeans. But there are a few differences Down Under.

Because the Southern Hemisphere is tipped toward the sun while the Northern Hemisphere is tipped away from it, their seasons are reversed: In the Southern

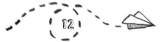

Hemisphere summer starts in December, and August is the depth of winter.

So an Australian Christmas doesn't have sleigh rides and chestnuts roasting on an open fire—it's more likely to involve a barbecue and a trip to the beach!

The moon is upside down in the Southern Hemisphere too: The Man in the Moon's eyes are at the bottom, and a waning (shrinking) crescent looks like this.

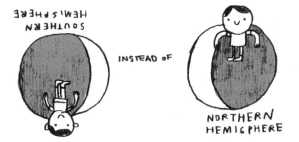

SOUTHERN HEMISPHERE

INSTEAD OF

NORTHERN HEMISPHERE

One thing that's not different in the Southern Hemisphere: going to the bathroom! It's sometimes said that toilets flush counterclockwise in the Northern Hemisphere and clockwise in the Southern, but that's not true. There *is* a force called the Coriolis effect that makes big things, like weather systems, rotate differently in the two hemispheres, but a toilet is just too small to be affected.

East Is East and West Is West

Latitude at sea is pretty easy. Since ancient times, sailors have known how to judge their latitude from the height of the sun at noon. All you need to know is the date.

Longitude, however, was a lot harder. Today, we're used to having GPS devices in our cars and phones, so it's hard for us to understand that, just 250 years ago, there was *no invention on Earth* that could tell you how far west or east you were at any given time! Mostly, sailors had to guess about longitude and hope for the best.

In 1717, a terrible shipwreck off the coast of England sank four ships and killed over fourteen hundred sailors, including the heroic British admiral of the fleet Sir Cloudesley Shovell.

Junior Genius Joviality!

The next time you have a substitute teacher, make sure to tell the sub your name is Sir Cloudesley Shovell!

Shovell's fleet, it turned out, had run aground because they'd calculated their longitude wrong. As a result of the disaster, the British government offered a £20,000 prize (over a million dollars in today's money!)

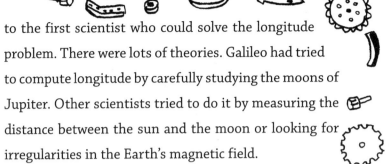

to the first scientist who could solve the longitude problem. There were lots of theories. Galileo had tried to compute longitude by carefully studying the moons of Jupiter. Other scientists tried to do it by measuring the distance between the sun and the moon or looking for irregularities in the Earth's magnetic field.

The problem was finally solved with, of all things, a really good clock. Why a clock? Well, if you know what time the sun is supposed to set today back home in London, and you can tell what time the sun just set at your current location, then you know how far west or east of London you are. Unfortunately, good eighteenth-century clocks all used a swinging pendulum, which means they didn't keep reliable time when a ship was bouncing around on a stormy sea. A clock maker named John Harrison solved this problem by inventing a clock that could keep accurate time on the waves, and he collected a hefty prize and died a very wealthy man.

Extra Credit

Before an international conference decided that the "zero" line of latitude, the prime meridian, would run through Greenwich, England, many maps used a meridian through Paris. In 1994, the city of Paris marked that old meridian—which still shows up on some French maps, even though everyone uses Greenwich today—with a string of 135 bronze medallions set into the ground. Not to be outdone, the Greenwich observatory installed a green laser that projects the prime meridian into the London sky every night.

Zoning Out

In 1884, a Canadian engineer named Sandford Fleming proposed dividing the world into twenty-four standard time zones, more or less the system we have today. At the time, there was no such thing as "standard time" in most countries. Until the 1880s, the United States alone was divided into more than eight thousand time zones, with each town setting its own local time based on the position of the sun at noon. This worked fine until railroads started to cross the country, and at that point thousands of time zones made train schedules *very* confusing.

The delegates at the conference decided not to institute Fleming's time zone system, leaving it up to

individual countries. Over the next fifty years, pretty much the whole world adopted some kind of "standard time" based on Fleming's system, giving us the time zone map we have today.

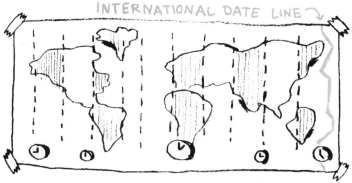

INTERNATIONAL DATE LINE

You probably already know that when it's noon on Monday in Los Angeles, it's three in the afternoon in New York City. This continues across the globe: It's already eight o'clock at night in London (so maybe the prime meridian laser just turned on at Greenwich). It's midnight in Moscow and 4 AM in China and western Australia—in other words, it's already tomorrow! At some point in our eastward journey, we need to jump back from tomorrow to today. That jump happens at the international date line, the zigzaggy line up there through the Pacific. On the west side of that line, it's 6 AM Tuesday. An inch to the right, on the east side, it's 7 AM . . . but on Monday.

This may seem silly, but what's the alternative? To have it be the same time (say, 8 AM Monday) all over the world, even if the sun is setting in Cairo and it's pitch-black in Tokyo? I'm sure you can agree, Junior Geniuses, that this would be even sillier.

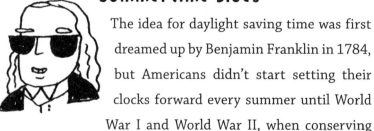

Blast from the Past

Because of time zones, it's quite possible to take off in an airplane and land at your destination at an earlier time than you left! Sportscaster Bob Costas likes to tell the story of traveling with a 1970s basketball team called the Spirits of St. Louis. The Spirits' colorful star, Marvin "Bad News" Barnes, took a look at his itinerary at the airport one day and saw that his flight was leaving Louisville at 8 PM and arriving in St. Louis at 7:56 PM due to the change from eastern to central time. "I ain't getting on no time machine!" Barnes told Costas, and walked off to rent a car instead.

Summertime Blues

The idea for daylight saving time was first dreamed up by Benjamin Franklin in 1784, but Americans didn't start setting their clocks forward every summer until World War I and World War II, when conserving

FALL BACK

SPRING FORWARD

daylight meant conserving precious fuel.

All that clock changing can cause confusion. Every autumn when clocks fall backward one hour, Amtrak trains find themselves an hour ahead of schedule midjourney, so they just stop on the tracks and chill for an hour! An even weirder case happened in a Cary, North Carolina, hospital in 2007, as Laura Cirioli gave birth to twins one November night. Her son, Peter, was born first, at 1:32 AM. But then the clocks moved back one hour to end daylight saving, and her second twin, Allison, was born thirty-four minutes later, at 1:06 AM. So she's technically twenty-six minutes older than her brother, who was born first!

Pop Quiz!

What's the only state in the Lower 48 states that doesn't observe daylight saving time?

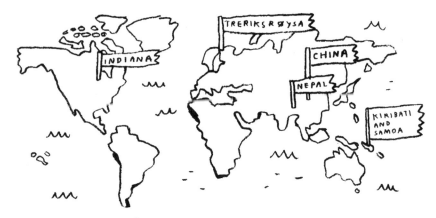

The World's Five Most Confusing Time-Zone Tangles

NEPAL. Most of the Earth's many time zones differ from Greenwich time by a certain whole number of hours: Brazil is three hours earlier, Ethiopia is five hours later. A few places are offset by a half-hour difference. But Nepal, in the Himalayas, is the only country with a fifteen-minute difference! That's right: When it's ten in India, it's ten fifteen next door in Nepal! That's because Nepal still uses its most sacred mountain, Gauri Sankar, as its own private meridian instead of adopting India's standard time. Locals call the fifteen-minute gap "Nepali stretched time" and use it as an excuse to be a little late for appointments.

KIRIBATI AND SAMOA. For its first fifteen years of independence, the Pacific island nation of Kiribati straddled both sides of the international date line, so it was always two different days at the same time in Kiribati! In 1995, it moved its remote eastern islands into the same time zone as its western half. Coincidentally—or not—this change makes eastern Kiribati the first nation on Earth to celebrate the New Year every year. This was a big tourist draw when the new millennium dawned on December 31, 1999!

TRERIKSRØYSA. There are about twenty places worldwide where three time zones meet at a single point. One of the weirdest is this spot on the border of Norway, Finland, and Russia. All three countries observe a different time zone, and Russia doesn't have daylight saving time. This means that, in the winter, you can walk west across the border just a few inches and go back in time four hours! When Norway's border guards come on duty at 8 AM, their Russian counterparts across the way are already breaking for lunch.

INDIANA. Of all the fifty states, Indiana has always been the one where it's hardest to answer the simple question "What time is it?" For half of the twentieth century, Indiana went back and forth on the question of daylight saving time. Often one town would set its clocks forward every spring, while the next town down the road wouldn't. Also, some Indiana counties would jump back and forth between central and eastern time every so often. Travelers might have to change their watches six or seven times driving across the state. It was a mess! Today there are eighty Indiana counties in eastern time, but twelve others have stuck with central time.

CHINA. China is really big—the third-largest nation on Earth in area and over three thousand miles wide. You'd expect it to span *five* of the world's conventional time zones. But the Chinese government, in a show of unity, has decreed since 1949 that the whole country, even though it's bigger than the United States, should all observe the same time zone: Beijing time. In other words, when it's 6:30 AM in Afghanistan, you could step across the border into western China and find that, even though the sun is just rising, it's technically ten o'clock already! You're late for work! As you might guess, many farms and communities just go by the sun and ignore the time Beijing tells them that it is.

Snow Time for That Now!

What time is it at the South Pole? The South Pole is where all time zones meet, so it really doesn't matter how you set your watch. The sun won't help: It stays up for six months out of the year, and then goes down for the other six months! Antarctic bases tend to keep their time based on the place their supplies and staff arrive from. The research base at the bottom of the world is called the Amundsen-Scott South Pole Station, and it's an American base where at least fifty people live year-round. Flights into Amundsen-Scott come from Christchurch, New Zealand, via America's McMurdo Station, so the South Pole observes New Zealand time.

SECOND PERIOD

Highs and Lows

The Earth is a remarkable place, Junior Geniuses. Unfortunately, much of what many people think they know about its geography is just not true. A geography book might tell you that Mount Everest is the tallest mountain on Earth, that the Sahara is the largest and hottest desert, that the Dead Sea is the lowest place on the Earth's surface not covered by the oceans.

All of this is dead wrong. Or at least it's not the full story.

Top of the World, Ma!

The great British explorer George Mallory said he wanted to climb Mount Everest "because it's there," so let's start with Everest. Certainly it's hard to miss, towering above the Himalayas at a lofty altitude of 29,035 feet above sea level. And it's growing! Geologic activity under the

Himalayas pushes Everest upward another 2.4 inches every year. This means that every single mountaineer who scales Everest reaches a new altitude record. But it also means that in twenty-six thousand years, Everest will be a mile higher than it is today! So you might want to get started now.

Round It Off

Nobody actually knew what the highest peak on Earth even *was* until 1856, when the British published their survey of India. They had measured Mount Everest to be 29,000 feet tall, exactly, but the head surveyor was afraid nobody would believe the suspiciously round number and added two extra feet. For years, Everest's height was listed in books as 29,002 feet.

Mount Everest is, indeed, the Earth's highest point above sea level. But it's not the Earth's tallest mountain, and it's not the point on the Earth that sticks out farthest into space. Now, now, everyone stay in your seats. I will explain.

Everest for Fish

Imagine a massive volcano, so big and heavy that it pushes the rock around it down a full *four miles* deeper into the Earth. This volcano rises over 33,000 feet from its base, dwarfing puny Everest.

This supervolcano isn't on Mars or in a video game. In fact, you might have walked on it. This volcano is Mauna Kea, the highest point on the island of Hawaii.

So why isn't Mauna Kea taller than Mount Everest? It is only 33,000 feet high *if you measure from its base*. Unfortunately, its base is at the bottom of the very deep Pacific Ocean, so most of its slopes are below sea level. Its altitude above sea level is only 13,800 feet, roughly half of Everest's height. Mount Everest sits on a plateau that's already 15,000 feet above sea level.

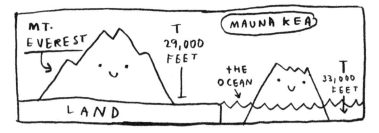

I Lied: The Earth Isn't Round

Another rival to Mount Everest's title is Mount Chimborazo in Ecuador. In our last lesson, you'll remember that we learned that the Earth is a round ball. Well, not exactly. It's not a perfect sphere, anyway.

Imagine yourself spinning on a merry-go-round. That pull you feel drawing you to the outside of the disk is called centrifugal ("sen-TRIFF-you-gull") force. Something similar acts on the Earth as it rotates, pulling mass very gradually toward the equator. As a result, over time, the Earth's poles have flattened and its middle section has gotten a little bit bulgy. So the Earth isn't a sphere anymore. It's closer to a shape scientists call an "oblate spheroid."

One result of this is that mountains near the equator are farther from the center of the Earth than are mountains at higher latitudes. So the tropical volcano called Chimborazo actually sticks out into space 7,000 feet farther than Everest, even though it's only 20,700 feet above sea level.

Extra Credit

Chimborazo isn't the only giant volcano in the Andes! If you were to list the world's sixty tallest volcanoes, *every single one* would be in South America.

Peak Condition

Despite this, Everest is still the gold standard for brave mountaineers. In fact, many climbers make it a goal to climb the Seven Summits: the highest points on all seven continents.

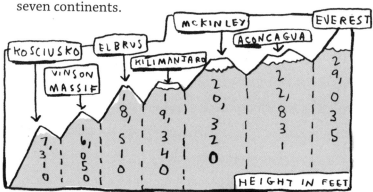

Climbers who have done all Seven Summits move on to the Explorers Grand Slam, which is *not* a breakfast platter. The Explorers Grand Slam is reaching all Seven Summits *and* the North and South Poles.

Extra Credit

None of these mountains, however, are as steep as Mount Thor, on Baffin Island in northern Canada. Its western face is a sheer cliff 4,100 feet high—a vertical drop of almost a mile! Thirty different teams failed at scaling it before a team finally got to the top in 1985. Their climb took thirty-three days!

But there are some downsides to all this explorer-ing. The north face of Mount Everest had never even been visited until 1921, but now it's pretty crowded up there. When the weather is good, people literally wait in line to start their climbs up and down, due to traffic along the trail. There's even phone coverage at the summit, thanks to a cell tower built at base camp in 2010! Discarded oxygen tanks are scattered all over the slopes, so an international cleanup effort is under way to get rid of the litter.

High Water Mark

What if you're a sailor instead of a mountain climber? What's the highest place on Earth you could take your ship? That would be a canal in southern Germany that connects two of Europe's most important rivers, the Rhine and the Danube. A series of locks lifts oceangoing boats to an elevation of 1,332 feet above sea level, almost as tall as Chicago's famous Sears Tower.

A Sinking Feeling

So what's the anti-Everest, the lowest point on Earth? That would be Challenger Deep, a valley in the Mariana

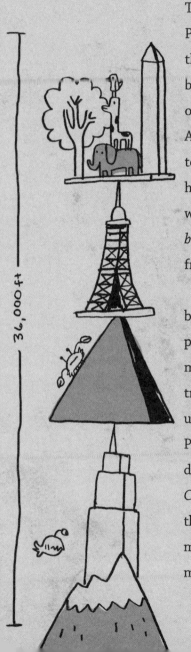

36,000 ft

Trench about 36,000 feet below the Pacific Ocean. I'd invite you down there, but there's no light to read by—it's pitch-black once you get just one-tenth of your way to the bottom! Also, the water pressure there is eight tons per square inch, so imagine a herd of the world's largest elephants, with one sitting on *each inch of your body*. You'd squish like a grape in a fraction of a second.

The Mariana Trench is so deep because it's a gap between two plates—the big shelves of rock that make up the Earth's crust. In the trench, the Pacific Plate is sinking under the neighboring Mariana Plate, forming a deep chasm. The deepest point is named for the HMS *Challenger*, the first boat to measure the ocean depths here. It carried 114 miles of weighted rope to make its measurements!

Extra Credit

Only three people have ever visited the bottom of Challenger Deep, using specially designed submersibles (deep-diving craft). The only person to do it since 1960 is James Cameron, the director of the movies *Avatar* and (of course!) *Titanic*.

If it's hard to imagine a 36,000-foot depth, try this. If you've ever been on an airplane, watching the tiny mountains and valleys pass by miles below, that's roughly the height that the surface of the Pacific lies above Challenger Deep!

Much of the ocean floor remains unmapped, so it's entirely possible that there's a deeper spot than Challenger Deep somewhere below the waves. For example, it wasn't until 1997 that scientists discovered another nearby part of the Mariana Trench called Sirena Deep, which is *almost* as deep as Challenger.

Low, But Not Low-Sodium

The lowest place on land is usually said to be the shores of the Dead Sea, between Israel, the West Bank, and Jordan, almost a third of a mile *below* sea level. *Unlike* the Mariana Trench, you can go for a nice swim there.

The water is so salty—over 30 percent salt!—that you'd float on the surface like you were wearing water wings.

There is, however, a place *much* lower than the Dead Sea that's not under the ocean. The Bentley Subglacial Trench, a vast valley in West Antarctica, goes down 8,300 feet below sea level. Technically, though, this trench *is* underwater—frozen water! There's a mile and a half of solid ice sitting on top of it.

Blizzards in the Desert

All that ice and snow make Antarctica seem like a pretty wet place, right? And everyone knows the world's largest desert is the Sahara, in North Africa. Both wrong, Junior Geniuses!

The Sahara is big, I'll give you that. It's roughly the size of the United States.

And though it was once a fertile grassland, it changed to an incredibly barren desert a few thousand years ago, probably because the Earth started tilting a little less in its rotation.

But it's not the biggest desert. Scientists define a desert as any place that gets less than ten inches or so of precipitation every year. It doesn't have to be hot, with camels and oases and whatnot. It just has to be dry. Antarctica is very dry, because it's too cold to snow much there. Believe it or not, Antarctica is by far Earth's biggest desert.

Extra Credit

The Sahara isn't even the Earth's biggest *sandy* desert— that's the Arabian Desert. Most of the Sahara is rocky and mountainous.

Hot Enough for Ya?

Until recently, the Sahara *was* believed to be the world's hottest place. A mining town called Dallol, in Ethiopia, recorded an average daily high temperature of 106°F for much of the twentieth century. That's a year-round *average*! And the highest temperature *ever* recorded was 136°F degrees, measured on September 13, 1922, by an Italian military fort at El Azizia, Libya.

In 2012, however, an international panel of weather experts studied that record more closely and decided that

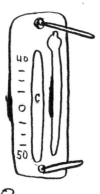

it was bogus: The temperature had been measured by a new observer on duty, and he'd just read his thermometer wrong!

So the official record is now 134°F, measured in Death Valley, California, in 1913.

Icy London, Icy France . . .

No place on Earth is as chilly as Antarctica, of course. In 1983, Russia's Vostok Station measured a temperature of -128.6°F. That's colder than dry ice!

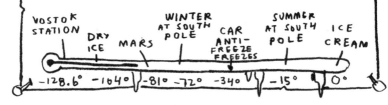

No Rain, No Gain

Even drier than the Sahara is the Atacama Desert in northern Chile, where just one millimeter of rain, on average, falls per year! That's about the thickness of a paper clip:

Scientists believe that, because the Atacama is located in the "rain shadow" between two mountain ranges, part of it hasn't seen a rainy day in 400 years, and riverbeds have been dry for 120,000 years!

The area is so dry and unearthly that NASA tests Mars landings there. The Atacama does support some life, though. Even in areas with little or no rainfall, a coastal fog called the *camanchaca* sometimes drifts in off the Pacific, supporting lichens and cacti that can "drink" moisture straight from the fog!

Pop Quiz!

The world's *wettest* spot is Mawsynram in the state of Meghalaya, which gets over eighty *feet* of rain every year, mostly during the monsoon season. What country do you think Mawsynram is in?

The Big Blue Diet

We've seen a lot of big numbers in this lesson, Junior Geniuses, but here's the biggest one of all: 6,585,000,000,000,000,000,000. That's the weight of the entire Earth in tons. (Well, the Earth is in a free-fall orbit, so technically its weight is zero. But something as massive as the Earth under the conditions we're used to would weigh 6.5 sextillion tons.)

If you think that's an awkwardly big number, I have some good news for you—its getting lower! That's right, the Earth is losing weight—about fifty thousand tons a year.

Even though a hundred tons of meteorites and other space dust fall to Earth every single day, twice that amount escapes out of our atmosphere in the form of hydrogen and helium gas.

The Lost Generation

Junior Geniuses: I hope learning about these extremes has reminded you that our planet is a big and interesting place. Unfortunately, a lot of people don't seem very interested in knowing about it. In National Geographic's most recent survey of college-age Americans:

○ *Only 79 percent could find the Pacific Ocean on a map.*

○ *Only 50 percent could find New York on a map.*

○ *Only 12 percent could find Afghanistan on a map.*

Geographic illiteracy, in other words, is a big problem.

The Reel World

Hollywood doesn't help much either. Take the case of *Krakatoa, East of Java*. This 1969 disaster movie depicted the famous 1883 eruption on the island of Rakata. It was even nominated for an Oscar. There's only one problem: Krakatoa is actually *west* of Java!

Here are a few more of my favorite geography goofs from the movies:

- JURASSIC PARK. The scene where Nedry, the evil computer nerd, agrees to smuggle out dinosaur embryos is set on a beach in San José, Costa Rica. But San José is located over fifty miles from the ocean!

- POCAHONTAS. The Disney princess manages to leap over a rocky thirty-foot cliff and plunge down a waterfall. But the movie is set on Virginia's coastal plain—a flat, marshy area with no mountains at all!

○ **ARMAGEDDON.** When the meteorite is destroyed, we see simultaneous celebrations all over the world, including America, India, and Turkey. Somehow, it's daytime in all those places!

○ **INDIANA JONES AND THE TEMPLE OF DOOM.** Flying southwest from Shanghai, Indy's plane passes over the Great Wall of China. That's a pretty good trick, since the wall is really hundreds of miles north!

○ **TITANIC.** Jack tells Rose he used to ice-fish on Wisconsin's Lake Wissota. He must have a time machine, since Lake Wissota was created by a dam in 1915, three years after the *Titanic* sank.

○ **ROBIN HOOD: PRINCE OF THIEVES.** Robin Hood arrives back in England by landing at the white cliffs of Dover, and gets to Nottingham later that day—even though that's a two-hundred-mile trip! He also passes Hadrian's Wall en route, which is odd, since that's up near Scotland.

∘ **THE SOUND OF MUSIC.** The Von Trapp family escapes over the Alps from Salzburg into neutral Switzerland. Unfortunately, the Swiss border is nowhere near Salzburg. Cross the border from Salzburg and you wind up in . . . Nazi Germany! Oops.

Geography is important, Junior Geniuses. I hope all of you will help educate the other people you know—even grown-ups—about geography. When we hear about far-away places in books or on the news, it's good to know a little bit about them. Just imagine a world where we all knew a little more about each other. Maybe then we wouldn't have to have wars and everyone would . . .

RECESS

What's that? You want to try some geography games during your morning break, Junior Geniuses? I have a few suggestions.

First and Last

In this classic geography game, players take turns giving place-names—cities, states, countries, oceans, mountains, and so forth. The catch is that the first letter of each place name must also be the *last* letter of the previous place named.

For example, if the first player says, "Arkansas," the second player needs to name a place that starts with an *S*, like Spain. The third player would then have to come up with a place that starts with *N*: New York City, for example. That's a tricky spot for the fourth player, who's forced to think of a place-name that starts with *Y*. Players are eliminated if they can't quickly produce an answer, and no place-name can be used more than once. The last player standing is the winner, and he or she begins the next game.

Treasure Map

Hide a "treasure" somewhere near where you're playing (or just draw an *X* in the dirt) and make a map for a group of friends. Don't give away everything—maybe just draw a few landmarks and add some tricky clues like "Walk twenty paces east of the tallest tree" or "Go halfway between the far soccer goal and the green fencepost, then turn left." See if your friends can follow the map to the secret destination. See if they can do it while you annoy them by talking like a pirate the whole time. Arrr!

THIRD PERIOD

Maps and Legends

When a baby loggerhead sea turtle hatches from its egg on a Florida beach, the first thing it does is hop into the ocean and swim northeast. The babies are only two inches long, can swim only about half a mile per hour, and can't even dive. But even though they're just hours old, they know exactly where they are. Baby loggerheads are born with the amazing ability to sense changes in the

Earth's magnetic field, so they always know which way to swim. If the baby turtle survives, it will spend the next decade making a giant circle, around the North Atlantic to Africa, before returning home to build its own nest.

No human can match that kind of seafaring feat, Junior Geniuses. When you were just born, you couldn't even roll over or hold your head up, much less swim the Atlantic. But humans have one navigational talent that no other species can match. We can pass along our geographic knowledge to others.

We can draw maps.

Putting the "Cart-" Before . . .

The French word for "map" is *carte*, so lots of English words used by map lovers begin with the prefix "cart-" or "carto-."

cartography	the study of maps
cartophile	a map lover
cartophobia	the fear of maps
cartifact	an object (postcard, toy, etc.) with a map drawn on it
cartocacoethes	the tendency to see maps everywhere

The English word "map," on the other hand, goes back to the Latin word *mapa*—meaning a napkin! Because early world maps were drawn on cloth, they were called *mappae mundi*, or "napkins of the world." This later got shortened to "map."

But that doesn't mean you should wipe your mouth on a map after eating barbecue.

O.G. (Original Geography)

A MAMMOTH TUSK
UKRAINE

Maps are older than written language, so we have no idea who drew the first map. The earliest

MAP ROCK, IDAHO

maps we know of don't look much like a modern road

atlas. They're usually part chart, part drawing, and part religious

CATAL HUYUK, TURKEY

artifact. These ancient maps predate paper, so they're carved in clay, painted on walls, or etched in rocks or even mammoth tusks.

BABYLONIAN CLAY TABLET

Extra Credit

Most people assume that atlases are named for Atlas, the Greek titan who held up the sky. Nope! They're actually named for a different mythological Atlas, an African king who supposedly invented the first globe.

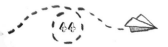

Scientists don't always agree on how to read these charts. Some people think the spotted shape in the Turkish mural opposite is a map of a nearby volcano. Others think it's just a picture of a leopard skin!

Here Be Dragons

For many centuries, European maps were a weird mix of geography and mythology, too. Engravers would often fill in the blank spaces on maps with bizarre creatures to make the map more interesting. (And also to make their boring jobs more interesting!)

In the far-off oceans, they drew an amazing variety of sea monsters attacking ships. Some were clearly based on whales. Others looked more like snakes, winged dragons, or even lions. The unexplored parts of Africa were often filled with half-human monsters: giants with six arms each, or just one eye, or the heads of dogs. These weren't only for decoration. People actually thought they'd find these crazy creatures in the far corners of the world!

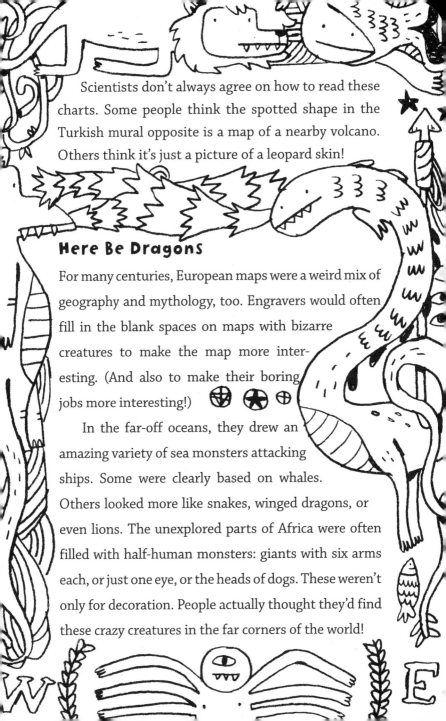

Extra Credit

Many people believe that old maps used the phrase "Here Be Dragons" to indicate the dangers of unknown places. In fact, no sea chart has *ever* been found that uses this phrase! The only place these words appear is an antique copper globe called the Hunt-Lenox Globe, today found in the New York Public Library.

On the Wrong Track

If you owned a world map in the Middle Ages, it would also be full of Bible stories. Jerusalem was assumed to be the geographic center of the world, since that was the holiest city for Christians. India would be located in the right place . . . but the Garden of Eden would be drawn right next door. The cities and coastline of Turkey would be very accurate . . . but Noah's ark would be sitting on one of the mountains there.

Today, it's funny to look back at some of the mistakes that stayed on maps for centuries. For about 150 years, Europeans believed that California was an island! The Spanish explorers who found the mouth of the

Colorado River proved that California was *not* an island in 1539, but as late as 1770, people were still drawing it that way on maps.

Junior Geniuses: If your family is planning a California vacation, *do not use these maps!* They are very inaccurate and also don't have Disneyland on them. But they are valuable! Collectors will pay tens of thousands of dollars for these mistaken maps at auctions.

The Ten-Million-Dollar Map

In 1901, the last remaining copy of a 1507 world map by a cartographer named Martin Waldseemüller was discovered in a castle tower in Germany. One hundred years later, the U.S. Library of Congress paid a whopping *$10 million* to buy it. Why is this the most expensive map in the world? Because it marks the first time that the name America was ever used to refer to the New World.

Flattening Will Get You Nowhere

It's easy to laugh at the mistakes on old maps, but today's state-of-the-art digital maps could never mislead us, right? Well, not so fast, Junior Geniuses. Here is still one of the most common maps of the world:

Greenland looks pretty big on this map at the left, doesn't it? Bigger than Africa, in fact. Would it surprise you to learn that Greenland is actually *smaller* than Africa? What if I told you that Greenland was smaller than Algeria, a *single country* in Africa?

This is a problem of "projections." The Earth is round (more or less), but a map is flat. So when we draw a map, we have to "project" its round continents and oceans onto a flat surface, squashing or stretching them to make them fit. Imagine trying to spread an orange peel into a flat rectangle and you'll see what I mean. It's hard.

The map above uses a kind of projection invented by a cartographer named Gerardus Mercator, the same guy who coined the word "atlas." The beauty of Mercator's

projection is that it preserves direction perfectly. Up on a Mercator map is always due north, left is due west, right is due east, and down is due south. Unfortunately, he accomplished this by totally screwing up area. That's why Greenland looks fourteen times bigger than it really is.

Left Out In the Cold

Another problem with a Mercator map: It's impossible to include the North and South Poles on one. Just can't be done. The paper would have to be *infinitely* tall before you got to the poles.

If you wanted to compare area more accurately, you could use a projection like the Gall-Peters, but then North Africa looks all stretchy and Alaska is squished.

You can't win.

The moral here, Junior Geniuses, is that any map, whether it's a Ukrainian mammoth tusk or a modern city map on a smartphone, is just one of

many possible ways of telling a story. When you look at a map, think about the story it tells.

Nowhere Fast

As proof that maps can't always be trusted, here are five places seen on maps that don't even exist in real life!

1. BARTLETT PLACE, LONDON. In 2005, it was revealed that a popular London street guide used this phony name for a real street, Broadway Walk. Why the fake name? Bartlett Place is a "trap street," a way for mapmakers to catch others who were stealing their facts. If "Bartlett Place" ever appears on another map, the publisher can prove that its data was copied.

2. AGLOE. This nonexistent town in the Catskill Mountains of New York was added to a 1930s road map as a copyright trap by Otto G. Lindberg and his assistant Ernest Alpers. ("Agloe" was coined by mixing up their initials, OGL and EA.) Many years later, a store was built at this spot, calling itself the Agloe General Store, in honor of the fake town!

3. BEATOSU AND GOBLU. A University of Michigan fan designing highway maps for Michigan in 1978 added these two made-up towns to nearby Ohio. Their names mean "Beat OSU!" and "Go Blue!" because Ohio State University is a big Michigan sports rival, and blue is one of Michigan's team colors.

4. THE LAND OF PARROTS, CAPE OF THE GOOD SIGNAL, AND SWEETEST RIVER.

When he compiled the very first world atlas in 1570, Abraham Ortelius wanted to include Terra Australis—a vast southern continent that many explorers had predicted but no one had ever seen—but didn't want to leave it empty. So he labeled its coast with all kinds of made-up names. Today, unfortunately, we know that none of these places are real, because Terra Australis doesn't exist.

5. ARGLETON.

This mysterious English town appeared on Google Maps for many years even though there's no village there in real life, just empty pasture. Where did Argleton come from? Where did it go? Nobody knows.

The Adventures of Supermap!

Maps sometimes have mistakes, but that doesn't mean they're not useful or powerful. Maps are an amazingly effective solution to one of the oldest and hardest problems ever to face human beings: How do we understand the parts of the world we can't see at the moment? After all, the horizon is only two or three miles away from us at all times. Maps help us find our way to places that our eyes just can't.

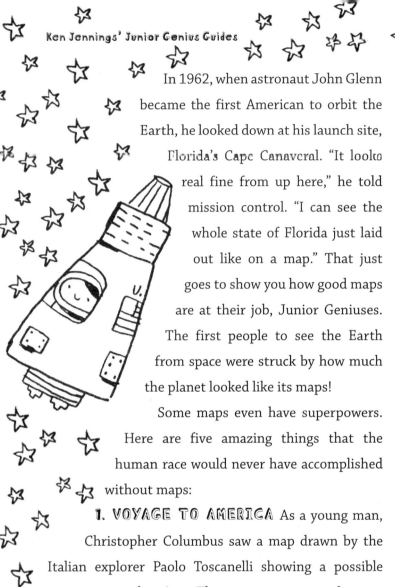

In 1962, when astronaut John Glenn became the first American to orbit the Earth, he looked down at his launch site, Florida's Cape Canaveral. "It looks real fine from up here," he told mission control. "I can see the whole state of Florida just laid out like on a map." That just goes to show you how good maps are at their job, Junior Geniuses. The first people to see the Earth from space were struck by how much the planet looked like its maps!

Some maps even have superpowers. Here are five amazing things that the human race would never have accomplished without maps:

1. VOYAGE TO AMERICA As a young man, Christopher Columbus saw a map drawn by the Italian explorer Paolo Toscanelli showing a possible route westward to Asia. The map was wrong, of course (America wound up being in the way), but it inspired Columbus's famous 1492 voyage.

2. CURE DISEASES. In 1854, an epidemic of a terrible disease called cholera hit London, killing more than six hundred people. People back then didn't know about germs—they thought that diseases were spread by "bad air." A doctor named John Snow studied the spread of the disease and realized that all the cases originated at one public water pump. The local council agreed to take the handle off the contaminated pump, and the outbreak ended. Snow drew a dot map of his study to help convince city authorities to solve the sewage problem that was contaminating the drinking water. That map was the beginning of the "germ" theory of disease.

3. FIGHT POVERTY. In the 1890s, census data showed that one in every four Londoners lived in terribly poor conditions. A businessman named Charles Booth doubted the real number was that high, so he organized his own survey of London, producing a color-coded map that marked city blocks in a rainbow of shades from black ("vicious, semi-criminal") to red ("middle class") to gold ("wealthy"). Booth was shocked to learn from his map that, in fact, the problem was worse than the government knew: A *third* of London lived below the poverty line. So he spent the rest of his life as an advocate for the poor.

4. WIN WORLD WAR II. You probably know about the heroic Allied troops that took the beaches of Normandy on D-day: June 6, 1944. But the invasion worked only because of the (also heroic!) cartographers who mapped those beaches in the months leading up to the invasion. First, British radio asked its listeners to send in their prewar holiday photos. Seven *million* postcards and snapshots of beach vacations poured in, and the Allies used all this photo evidence to begin their maps. Then they flew dangerous air missions over the coast and even stole ashore by night in wetsuits to map the beaches in amazing detail without the Germans ever catching on.

5. LAND ON THE MOON. In 1962, NASA began making maps of the moon's surface, to prepare for an eventual landing there. On July 20, 1969, Neil Armstrong and Buzz Aldrin had a pouch of these maps with them as their lunar lander, *Eagle*, approached the moon, and they looked out the small window to identify the craters and lava seas they were seeing. Just like John Glenn, they saw that the surface matched their maps exactly!

Earth Apples

Ever since people decided that the Earth was round (hundreds of years BC, as we already saw) they've been making spherical maps of the world too, called globes. The oldest surviving globe—made in Germany in 1492, while Columbus was sailing the Atlantic—is called the Erdapfel, or "earth apple."

Did you ever make a hollow piñata by slapping papier-mâché onto a balloon, and then popping the balloon inside? That's basically how the first globes were made: by wrapping papier-mâché onto a clay ball, and then slicing away the round shell once it had dried.

Today, globes are much easier to make.

1. Maps of the Northern and Southern Hemispheres, spread out into strips with the poles in the centers, are glued onto round sheets of cardboard.

2. Then they're cut out into pinwheel shapes.

3. The pinwheels get stuck on top of a round dome and are pushed up into a heated cavity, which presses them, like an iron, into round hemispheres.

4. These cardboard bowls are then glued and taped together at the equator and mounted on a pedestal.

Globes are big sellers when international events are in the news. After the Japanese attack on Pearl Harbor, Americans actually stood in line for hours to buy globes. Even today, almost a million globes are sold worldwide every year!

Five Huge Globes Worth Crossing the Globe to See

1. THE WORLD'S BIGGEST GLOBE. That would be Eartha in Yarmouth, Maine, the headquarters of the mapping company DeLorme. Eartha is forty-two feet tall—much higher than a football goalpost. Time passes a lot faster on Eartha than it does on Earth: It rotates once an hour, not just once a day.

2. THE GLOBE THAT UPDATES ITSELF EVERY DAY. Mitsubishi Electric's Geo-Cosmos, which hangs from the ceiling in Tokyo's Miraikan Museum, is a twenty-foot aluminum globe covered with 10,362 computer screens that show new images of the Earth every day: almost-live vegetation, ocean, and weather conditions.

3. THE GLOBE YOU CAN WALK THROUGH. Boston's Mapparium is a stained-glass globe three stories high—but with the continents drawn on the *inside*!

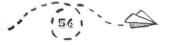

Visitors walk through the hollow globe on a catwalk. It's the only place on Earth where you can see the entire planet, in perfect perspective, without having to take a single step.

4. THE GLOBE OWNED BY THE WORST PERSON EVER. Adolf Hitler loved giant globes. The Volkswagen-size one in Berlin's German Historical Museum is one of the Columbus Globes that Hitler provided for all high-ranking Nazi officials. It has a bullet hole through Germany, made by the ticked-off Russian soldier who recaptured the globe at the end of World War II.

5. THE GLOBE YOU CAN GO ON VACATION IN. An eccentric oil billionaire called the Rainbow Sheikh owns an amazing collection of custom-made giant vehicles, which he keeps in a pyramid-shaped warehouse in the desert outside Abu Dhabi. My favorite is a spherical eight-bedroom trailer forty feet tall that's a perfect replica of the Earth—at exactly one-millionth its actual size.

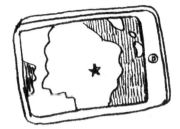

The New World

Today, of course, the coolest globes are digital ones that you browse on the Web. Google Earth, for example, has been downloaded one *billion* times! One-seventh of humanity could be looking at Google Earth *right now*.

With these new geo-browsers, you can do lots of things that old cardboard globes and paper maps just can't. Fly around the skyscrapers of Shanghai in 3-D, or zoom through the Grand Canyon like a hawk. Watch weather and traffic move across your neighborhood. Look at photographs of almost any city street in the world—or of the glaciers of Antarctica, the paintings of Russia's Hermitage Museum, or shipwrecks on the ocean floor. The aerial images these applications use are so detailed that when I look at my backyard, I can even see my Labrador retriever, Banjo, standing guard!

So many people are now exploring Google Earth that lots of cool things get discovered there *before* people actually find them on real Earth! It's called "armchair archaeology," and here's a partial list of the digital discoveries:

Giant "geoglyphs" (or ground drawings) in Peru

 Fossil caves in South Africa

 Medieval forts in Afghanistan

 Meteorite craters in Egypt and Australia

 Roman ruins in Italy and Britain

A lost mountain jungle in Mozambique—which turned out to be southern Africa's largest rain forest and home to hundreds of newly discovered species!

The most surprising result may be the one from a team of German scientists who used Google Earth to count 8,510 cows and 2,974 deer grazing in pastures. They found that most of the animals line up north–south to graze—the first proof that large mammals have a built-in compass to sense the Earth's magnetic field. People had been watching cows eat grass for thousands of years, but nobody ever noticed which way they were facing until we checked Google Earth!

Extra Credit

Did you know that looking at maps can make your brain bigger? In a 2000 study, scientists scanned the brains of London taxi drivers who had passed a very difficult geography test about the city's streets by studying maps. Each cabbie's hippocampus—the part of the brain that helps us navigate—was actually physically larger than that of a normal Londoner.

Off the Charts

Some of the most elaborately drawn maps even depict places that don't exist! Whole atlases have been published of fictional places like the starship *Enterprise* or J. R. R. Tolkien's Middle-earth. This makes sense, since many writers are just like Columbus: They get their best ideas from looking at maps.

When Stephenie Meyer began writing the *Twilight* books, she had never been to Forks, Washington, the town where the books are set. She just did an Internet search for places rainy enough to be vampire-friendly and chose Forks almost at random. But let me tell you a secret: Some of the strangest made-up settings you can think of are actually real places in disguise!

Fictional Spot	Clearly Based on	How to tell
Kanto (from Pokémon video games)	The Kantō Plain, Japan	The name is the same, and so is the coastline. Celadon City and Saffron City, Kanto's biggest cities, represent Tokyo, while the sea-port of Vermilion City is nearby Yokohama.
Prydain (from Lloyd Alexander novels like *The Black Cauldron*)	Wales	The Great Avren river in the Chronicles of Prydain series is based on the real-life River Severn, while the River Ystrad is the Wye. "Prydain" sounds exotic, but it's actually just the Welsh word for "Britain."
Metropolis (from Superman comics)	New York City	It sits on a Manhattan-shaped island called New Troy. There's a West River instead of the East River, a Centennial Park instead of Central Park, a Lacey's department store where Macy's should be, and so on.
The Hundred Acre Wood (from Winnie-the-Pooh)	Ashdown Forest, England	Travel to this East Sussex forest and check out the signs and plaques pointing out the sites there that inspired A. A. Milne's Pooh books. Milne had a country home there, and his son, Christopher Robin, would often play with his stuffed animals in the forest nearby.

ART CLASS

As we learned this morning, Junior Geniuses, "cartocacoethes" is the tendency to see maps everywhere—a mud puddle that looks like Australia, a piece of lasagna that looks like Oregon. But what about the opposite: looking at a map and seeing shapes of *other* things?

There is a long tradition of seeing shapes on maps. In the sixteenth century, mapmakers from Belgium and the Netherlands first drew the Leo Belgicus, reimagining the Low Countries as a noble lion.

THE LOW COUNTRIES

—LION—

Italy, it's often been noticed, looks like a boot.

ITALY

—BOOT—

Korea has been drawn as a tiger clawing at Manchuria.

Thailand, where the elephant is sacred, actually looks a lot like an elephant head.

Slovenians call their country Mother Chicken . . . for obvious reasons!

Do you ever look at a map and think that, hey, Cuba looks like a moustache, or the Lower Peninsula of Michigan is a mitten? For today's art project, choose the state or country where you live, or one you've traveled to or would like to visit. Trace its outline on a separate piece of paper. Then make a drawing of whatever you like by filling in the outline. Can you get a friend or a grown-up to guess what map inspired your drawing?

FOURTH PERIOD

The Watery Part of the World

The ocean is the last unexplored frontier on our planet. Seven-tenths of the Earth's surface are covered by water, but less than 10 percent of the ocean has been mapped. In fact, our charts of the ocean floor are *fifteen times* less detailed than our maps of the moon and Mars!

Deep Trouble

Our lack of ocean exploration means that there are still lots of mysteries left to be uncovered in the depths of the sea. For centuries, sailors traded stories of a horrific sea monster, one so scary that it probably inspired the kraken of Viking legend and the tentacled ship-wrecking menace Scylla in Greek myth. But few had ever seen these creatures' twenty-foot tentacles—only the circular

sucker scars left on the skin of the sperm whales they battled. In fact, the first images of a live giant squid weren't taken by scientists until 2004! A creature longer than a school bus was living right under our boats this whole time, and it took us thousands of years to actually see it swimming.

The ocean is so vast that nobody really knows what's down there. Scientists had always assumed that a fish called the coelacanth ("SEE-luh-kanth") had been extinct since the age of the dinosaurs. But in 1938, a South African fisherman hauled in his catch, and there was a coelacanth, still alive and kicking. In 2006, oceanographers conducting a Census of Marine Life (using radar, sonar, and robots!) announced that *Neoglyphea neocaledonica*, a five-inch shrimp with red spots and big eyes, had been found a mile beneath the surface of Australia's Coral Sea. This shrimp was thought to have been extinct for 50 million years!

"The age of discovery is not over!" said one of the scientists overseeing

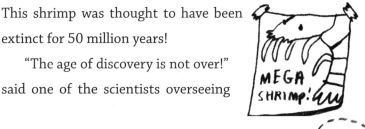

MEGA SHRIMP!

the census. That project also counted 230,000 different species in the ocean so far, but some scientists think there could be as many as 10 *million* undiscovered species still swimming around down there. In 2012, a French research ship called the *Tara* spent two years studying microscopic sea critters and found over a million new species of plankton alone!

Survivors

Scientists used to assume that the unexplored depths of the sea harbored little life, since there's not even sunlight down there. But today we know that, no matter how lousy the neighborhood, *someone* will want to move in. Even in pitch-black water three miles down, food chains form around hydro-thermal vents—smoking pits of lava-heated water. They're good places to hang out if you want to meet blind crabs, snails covered in iron scales, and six-foot-long tube worms.

Even in zero-degree water six hundred feet beneath the Antarctic ice sheets, shrimp and jelly-fish live happily. Life always finds a way.

How Many Oceans?

You may have heard of ships "sailing the seven seas," but take a look at a globe: There are actually more than one hundred different seas. The ancients never really agreed on what the so-called seven seas actually were. Each culture had its own list:

Phoenician	Arabian	Medieval
Adriatic Sea	Bay of Bengal	Adriatic Sea
Aegean Sea	Gulf of Khambhat	Arabian Sea
Alboran Sea	Gulf of Thailand	Black Sea
Balearic Sea	Persian Gulf	Caspian Sea
Ionian Sea	Singapore Strait	Mediterranean Sea
Ligurian Sea	South China Sea	Persian Gulf
Tyrrhenian Sea	Strait of Malacca	Red Sea

Homework

Can you find all these seas on a map or globe?

You might notice that the actual *oceans* are totally missing from these lists. (Oceans are typically bigger than seas, and less enclosed by land.) Some world maps today do indeed show the oceans as "seven seas" by dividing the Atlantic and Pacific into two each (North and South Pacific, North and South Atlantic), but the International Hydrographic Organization, the group that oversees water mapping, long used a list of just four oceans: the Pacific (by far the biggest), the Atlantic, the Indian, and the Arctic (by far the smallest).

Extra Credit

The oceans contain almost one-third of a *billion* cubic miles of water. That means you could empty them into a big cube of water 684 miles on each side! (If you needed a *really deep* swimming pool for some reason.)

In 2000, the IHO shook everything up by actually *creating a new ocean*! Every nation in its survey (except Argentina) agreed that a fifth ocean should be added to maps: the Southern Ocean, surrounding Antarctica. This new ocean is carved out of the southernmost reaches of what used to be the Pacific, Atlantic, and Indian Oceans.

Of course, there's no one right way to divide up the Earth's seas. Check a map: All these oceans and seas connect with one another. So the truth is that, for billions of years, the Earth has really only had one big ocean.

Sea Change

But that doesn't mean that the oceans have always looked the way they do today. Take a trip back in time with me, Junior Geniuses. (Don't worry about dinosaurs. We carry insurance.) During the Paleozoic Era, when all Earth's continents were stuck together in one big land mass called Pangaea, the surrounding ocean was called Panthalassa.

Later, when Pangaea began to split apart into super-continents like Gondwana and Laurasia, the gap that opened between them was called the Tethys Sea.

Extra Credit

These primeval oceans were named for Thalassa and Tethys, two different Greek sea goddesses.

This process continues today. The Earth's continents move, as we've seen, because they're sitting on separate tectonic plates of rock. These large plates meet at the bottom of the oceans, and where the seafloor is slowly spreading apart between plates, lava rushes up to fill in the gap, solidifying over time into tall underwater ridges.

As a result, Europe and North America are moving away from each other at an incredibly slow rate—just

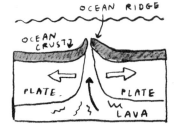

over an inch every year. That's about the same rate your fingernails grow!

Did you know that Alaska and Russia *almost* touch over on the other side of North America? Until about ten thousand years ago, a land bridge connected the Bering Strait, allowing migration of people and animals across what is now sixty miles of icy ocean.

Across the Sea

Russia and Alaska might one day be connected again! Since the nineteenth century, business and government leaders have dreamed of building a passage across the Bering Strait. Because there are two islands, the Diomedes, in the middle of the strait, the continents could be connected, for example, by a pair of twenty-five-mile bridges. Those are long bridges, but they wouldn't be the world's longest. (China's Jiaozhou Bay Bridge, at 25.8 miles, is currently longer.) Imagine being able to hop in your car and drive from Los Angeles all the way to Hong Kong! You could even drive from New York to London, but it would be a *loooong* way around.

In 2011, the Russian government set aside $65 billion to build a rail tunnel under the strait, so this centuries-old dream may actually come true someday. The tunnel would cross the international date line, so the west side would always be one day ahead of the east side—don't forget to change your watch *and* your calendar!

But the next time we redraw our ocean maps, plate tectonics won't be to blame. Ocean levels are projected to rise a foot or two over the next century, enough to put much of the Netherlands, Bangladesh, the Maldives, and other low-lying countries underwater. If the glaciers of Greenland and West Antarctica follow, sea levels could go up twenty feet or more. That would cause millions of square miles of flooding, in places ranging from Louisiana to southern Vietnam to northeastern Italy to Shanghai. If you plan on living in a coastal city in the next century, bring your scuba mask.

Pop Quiz!

The world's highest tides—upwards of fifty feet!—are found in the Bay of Fundy. The Bay of Fundy is between New Brunswick and Nova Scotia in what country?

◺◿◢◺◯◺

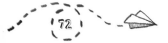

The Big Blue Eye

The largest of the Earth's oceans is the Pacific Ocean, stretching between the Americas, Asia, and Australia.

It covers almost 70 million square miles—that's about the same as all the other oceans put together. All the Earth's land area, all seven continents, could float in the Pacific Ocean and even have room left over.

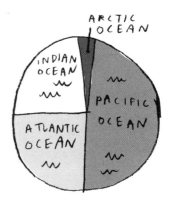

Movers and Shakers

The Pacific Ocean rests on the world's largest tectonic plate, the Pacific Plate, and its circular boundary is the most volcanically violent area in the world. Geologists call it the Ring of Fire, because about 90 percent of the world's earthquakes and 75 percent of its volcanoes are located there. The earthquakes of Japan, the volcanoes of the Andes, the San Andreas Fault—all part of the Ring of Fire.

So you won't be surprised when I tell you that the two most violent earthquakes ever recorded—one in Chile in 1960 and another near

Anchorage, Alaska, in 1964—both took place on the Ring of Fire. The Chilean earthquake was a 9.5 on the Richter scale—forty times stronger than the earthquake that leveled San Francisco in 1906. Rivers changed courses that day, and landslides moved whole mountains. The Alaska quake actually lifted part of the coastline 82 feet into the air permanently, and created tsunamis that caused drownings as far away as California!

The Heart of the Ocean

The Pacific Ocean is also where you'd find Point Nemo, the spot on the world's oceans that is farthest from land. Named for Captain Nemo, the submarine captain in Jules Verne's *Twenty Thousand Leagues Under the Sea*, Point Nemo is located in the middle of the South Pacific, 1,670 miles away from the nearest bit of land on all sides: the Pitcairns, the Easter Islands, and the Antarctic coast. Better start swimming!

Thousand Island Stressing

The Pacific Ocean contains more than twenty-five thousand islands, from the world's second-largest island (New Guinea) to its smallest island nation (Nauru, so small that its only airport runway stretches all the way across the island)!

Extra Credit

The world's largest island, if continents don't count, is Greenland. But that's probably only because it's so cold there. Scientists think that if we could ever magically remove Greenland's massive ice cap, we might find out that there are actually three separate islands under there, not one big one.

What's the smallest island? That one is a little tougher. Does a rock in a puddle count? According to *The Guinness Book of World Records*, the world's smallest island *with a building on it* is Bishop Rock, at the western end of the English Channel. This little spike of rock covers .0002 square miles—one-tenth of an acre, about the size of a backyard garden—and every inch of it is covered with a stone lighthouse built in 1858.

Until 1992, this island was also the world's smallest inhabited island, but today the lighthouse is automated.

Some of the world's most exotic vacation spots are islands, but let me warn you about a few islands you probably *don't* want to visit.

○ ILHA DE QUEIMADA GRANDE, BRAZIL. This island sits less than ninety miles off the coast of São Paulo, Brazil, one of the Earth's biggest cities. Unfortunately, the Brazilian navy bans tourists. Why? Because this is the only home of the golden lancehead viper, one of the world's most venomous snakes. Locals say there are about five of the deadly snakes for every square meter of the island!

○ **FERDINANDEA.** This is a volcanic island in the Mediterranean that appears above the waves every few centuries before getting submerged again. When it last appeared, in 1831, Britain, Sicily, France, and Spain all wanted Ferdinandea and starting arguing over who should control it—but the tiny chunk of basalt disappeared before they could figure it out. In 1986, American pilots mistook Ferdinandea for a Libyan submarine and dropped bombs on it!

○ **BOUVET ISLAND.** This Norwegian nature reserve in the South Atlantic is more than one thousand miles from land. It's not deserted, however; one hundred thousand penguins live there!

○ **MIYAKE-JIMA.** Since a 2000 volcanic eruption on this Japanese island, the ground has been continuously leaking poisonous sulfuric gas. Residents are required to carry gas masks around with them at all times.

○ **THILAFUSHI.** This artificial island in the Maldives, an archipelago in the Indian Ocean, was created to be the national garbage dump. More than 330 *tons* of trash are brought there every day, which means the floating garbage island is growing at the rate of one square meter every day.

Saline Away

The ocean, you may have heard, is salty—3 percent salt on average, more or less. That's enough salt to cover all the dry land on Earth with five hundred feet of salt, a layer about as tall as the Washington Monument! But that's an average: The ocean is not all *equally* salty. Over a thousand years ago, early Polynesians were able to explore the vast Pacific Ocean by tasting seawater and detecting tiny changes in its temperature and salinity (saltiness). Warmer, fresher water meant that an island was near.

Today the Red Sea is the saltiest open sea in the world, since surface water evaporates quickly in the hot climate and few freshwater rivers empty into it. During the rainy season in South America, on the other hand, the Amazon carries so much water into the Atlantic that you can sail one hundred miles out to sea, dip a bucket overboard, and drink fresh water straight from the ocean!

Ice Wide Open

Earlier, we learned about the Dead Sea, a lake so salty that even nonswimmers can float. Here's something not many people know, Junior Geniuses: The Dead  Sea is *not* the saltiest lake on Earth. Many of the lakes in Antarctica's McMurdo Dry Valleys are saltier than the Dead Sea, but one of them—tiny Don Juan Pond—is so salty that it doesn't even freeze over in the dead of the Antarctic winter! The water there is eighteen times saltier than the ocean.

Sodium chloride isn't the only thing dissolved in seawater, of course. The oceans also contain lots of magnesium, calcium, potassium, and many other minerals—including silver, platinum, and gold! A cubic mile of ocean water contains almost three ounces of

gold—but there's no way to extract it that won't cost more than the gold is worth. If there were, we could use the oceans to give *five pounds of gold* to every man, woman, and child on Earth!

A Tale of Two Lakes

The Caspian "Sea" between Kazakhstan and Iran isn't a sea at all—but it's so big that the ancient people who lived on its shores called it an ocean. Today, we know that it's actually the world's biggest lake. In fact, it contains almost half of all the world's lake water!

Just east of the Caspian Sea is another lake called the Aral Sea. For thousands of years, the Aral Sea was the world's fourth-largest lake. But in the 1960s, the Soviet Union diverted most of the area's rivers to irrigate crops, and the lake started to shrink. Today the lake is less than 10 percent of its original size, leaving a sandy desert where fishing boats now sit stranded. The secretary-general of the United Nations has called the Aral Sea "one of the world's worst environmental disasters."

But another remarkable Asian lake is thriving. Lake

Baikal, in Siberia, is the world's oldest freshwater lake as well as the deepest, more than a mile down in some spots! In the summer, the water is so clear that you can see down more than 130 feet.

Lake Baikal holds 20 percent of all the planet's fresh water—and it's getting bigger. That's enough drinking water to last everyone on Earth for fifty years.

"Current" Events

What's the longest river in the world? That's actually a hard question to answer. How far into the mountains do you find the "start" of a river? And where does its mouth end and the ocean begin?

Africa and South America both have claims to the "World's Longest River" title. It's definitely a close call, but the most recent discoveries may give the

AMAZON 4,225 MILES

NILE 4,132 MILES

YANGTZE 3,915 MILES

MISSISSIPPI 2,350 MILES

Amazon an edge over the Nile. In 2007, a Brazilian expedition found a new farthest source for the Amazon: an icy Peruvian volcano called Mismi. If this finding is correct, it means the Amazon is 4,225 miles long, winning by just ninety-three miles!

And here's one more surprising discovery from recent Amazon expeditions: The giant river used to run backward! By looking at flow patterns left in the rock, scientists now know that, during the Cretaceous Period, the Amazon used to flow west. Then volcanic activity raised up the Andes, and the river reversed directions!

Extra Credit

The world's tallest uninterrupted waterfall is usually said to be Angel Falls in Venezuela, more than half a mile high. But that's not 100 percent true. There's actually a much taller waterfall below the ocean between Greenland and Iceland. Cold, dense water from the Denmark Strait plunges over two miles straight down as it flows south into the Irminger Current. But should a waterfall really count if it's already underwater?

All right, Junior Geniuses, there's the bell. Let's line up for lunch.

LUNCH

Today, you can get a lesson in geography just by walking through a supermarket or food court. You'll see French fries, Chinese chicken salad, Greek yogurt, and Swiss cheese. But many of those names are misleading. "Russian dressing" was actually invented in New Hampshire. "Spanish rice" is a Tex-Mex dish that no Spaniard would recognize. And "German chocolate cake" has nothing to do with Germany at all. It's named after an American candy maker, Sam German!

But sometimes these local specialties come from exactly where they say they do. In Sweden, Swedish meatballs are just called . . . meatballs. More creatively, the French call French toast *pain perdu*, or "lost bread," because it's a way to reclaim bread that otherwise would have gone stale. Canadians call Canadian bacon "back bacon," because it's cut from the back of the pig. And Danishes aren't really Danish: In Denmark, they call that kind of pastry a *wienerbrød*, meaning "Viennese bread."

Here's a truly global lunch or snack idea that you can try anytime:

Mappetizers

Blue food coloring

Sour cream

1 large flour tortilla per mapmaker

Refried beans

Guacamole

Shredded cheddar and Monterey Jack cheese

1 pound lean ground beef with 1 taco seasoning mix (optional)

Crumbled tortilla chips (optional)

Directions

1. Add a few drops of food coloring to your sour cream until it mixes into a rich blue color. Spread the blue sour cream thinly over your tortilla. This makes your globe's oceans.

2. Now it's time to draw the map on top of your oceans! Use blobs of your taco toppings to suggest continents—either the ones from our Earth or from a fantasy planet of your choice. An atlas or Google Earth might inspire you. Use refried beans for brown areas like grasslands, and guacamole for green forests. Sprinkle the deserts with yellow cheese and the polar ice caps with white cheese.

If you want texture—mountain ranges, for example—ask a grown-up for help browning the ground beef with the taco mix, and then spoon it on where you want mountains. For a quicker option, use bits of tortilla chips instead.

Take a quick picture of your creation, and then devour the entire planet like a hungry comic-book monster.

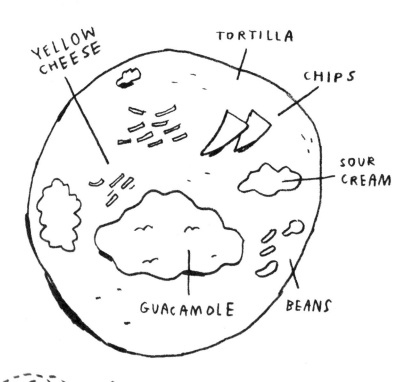

FIFTH PERIOD

From Afghanistan to Zimbabwe

Astronauts looking back at the Earth from space see one big blue planet. "We fly over most of the world, and you don't see borders," Mark Kelly, the captain of the space shuttle *Endeavour*, said in 2011.

Down here on Earth, of course, things are different. The Earth's 57 million square miles of land are divided into almost two hundred different countries, representing different nationalities and cultures. Some are huge, some are tiny. Russia is so big that it's always daytime there—by the time the sun sets in St. Petersburg, it's already rising on the other side of the country, in eastern Siberia! On the other extreme, Vatican City, the headquarters of the Roman Catholic Church, is a tiny independent state located entirely within the city of Rome, Italy. You could walk from one side of the country to the other in ten minutes!

There are 193 members of the United Nations today, running the alphabet from Afghanistan to Zimbabwe. Afghanistan has been the first nation alphabetically since 1931, when Abyssinia officially changed its name to Ethiopia. Zimbabwe has been the world's last country alphabetically since 1979, when it changed its name from Rhodesia. Before that, its African neighbor Zambia was in last place.

Today, there are countries that begin with every letter of the English alphabet except for *W* and *X*. (Western Samoa ruined everything by changing its name to Samoa in 1997.)

Homework

How many of the other twenty-four letters can you think of a country for? Here are a few to get you started: Algeria, Belgium, China . . .

Capital Ideas

Every country in the world has an official capital city where its government is headquartered. In some tiny countries, like Vatican City, Monaco, and Singapore, the country itself *is* its own capital city. Some capitals, like Tokyo and Mexico City, are megalopolises. A megalopolis is not a giant robot or dinosaur-monster, the way it might sound. It's just a sprawling cluster of different cities all mushed together.

Other capitals are smaller— like Thimphu, Bhutan, the world's only capital city without a single traffic light! In this Himalayan kingdom, intersections are still staffed by cops directing traffic with dancelike hand gestures. One traffic light  was installed a few years back, but locals (including the king!) complained, and a few days later, the signal was gone and the policemen were back on the job.

The lone exception is the tiny Pacific island of Nauru, which has no official capital. Yaren, the island's largest settlement with a population of only 1,100 people, serves as the unofficial capital. There you'll find its parliament house and the airport, where the national airline, Our Airline, landed its only plane until 2005, when the jet was repossessed by Australian creditors

Nauru See It, Nauru Don't

When Nauru became independent in 1968, it was the richest country on Earth due to its valuable deposits of phosphates—minerals from seabird droppings that are used to make fertilizers. But the bird-poop billions didn't last. Once all the phosphates had been strip-mined away, the country sank into poverty. Today, the unemployment rate there is 90 percent, and the obesity rate is even higher, due to the introduction of Western fast food during the phosphate boom. Nauru's latest idea to stay afloat: rebrand itself as a prison! In exchange for Australian aid, the tiny republic accepts thousands of refugees seeking political asylum in Australia. On the plus side, Nauruan is the only nationality on the planet that's a palindrome. (That means it's spelled the same forward and backward.)

You'd think one capital would be enough for anyone, Junior Geniuses, but some countries have two. In Bolivia, for example, the president and parliament both govern from the nation's largest city, La Paz. At an elevation of more than two miles above sea level, this makes it the highest capital city on Earth! But the Bolivian constitution says the official capital is actually Sucre, 435 miles southeast, where the country's supreme court meets.

Extra Credit

Despite a population of more than 2 million people, the La Paz area has only one fire station, and fires there are almost unheard of. Why? At twelve thousand feet up, there's barely enough oxygen in the air to start a fire.

In the Netherlands, Amsterdam is used for royal occasions like weddings and coronations, so it's the official capital. But the country has been governed from a different city, The Hague, for more than four hundred years!

South Africa effectively has *three* capitals, as a result of a nation-building compromise in 1910. The president governs from Pretoria, the parliament meets in Cape Town, and the Supreme Court of Appeal hands down decisions in Bloemfontein.

You'd think one of these countries with multiple capitals could donate one to poor Nauru.

Indian Summer

In centuries past, both India and Afghanistan split the year between "summer" and "winter" capitals. Every spring, the government would move to higher elevations to escape the brutal summer heat, then head south in autumn before it got snowed in. In fact, India's northernmost state, Jammu and Kashmir, still observes this split. From May to October, its state capital is Srinagar; from October to May, it's the city of Jammu. This is called the Darbar Move, and it's an expensive tradition dating back to 1872, but it helps keep the peace between the state's two main regions.

Do It Yourself!

When Sargon II took over Assyria, he began building a brand-new capital modestly called Dur Sharrukin, the Fortress of Sargon, along the Tigris River. (He was killed in battle while the city was still being built, and it was never completed.) Russian tsar Peter the Great captured the Swedish fort of Nyenskans in 1703, built a huge new palace and city on the spot, and called it St. Petersburg. Even Washington, D.C., was mostly empty, marshy wetlands in 1790 when it was chosen to be America's capital. (The first two presidents, George Washington and John Adams, mostly governed from Philadelphia.)

Since the twentieth century, there's been a boom of nations moving their capitals out to the middle of nowhere. In 1909, Australia announced the new city of Canberra as its capital site, ending a long battle between Sydney and Melbourne over which of those two cities would be capital. The design for the new city was left up to an international contest, which was won by Walter Burley Griffin, the same American architect famous for inventing the carport!

WALTER GRIFFIN

In 1960, Brazil moved its capital inland from over-crowded Rio de Janeiro to a brand-new inland city called Brasilia. Downtown Brasilia, to symbolize its modernity, was built in the shape of an airplane.

Pop Quiz!

Can you name the world's northernmost national capital? It has a name meaning "Smoke Bay," because of all of its geysers and hot springs.

Some world capitals are pretty easy to remember. Others, though, would stump a spelling bee champ. Here, I'll say the ones on the left and you try to say the ones on the right.

Easy to Remember	Tongue Twister
Djibouti, Djibouti	Antananarivo, Madagascar
Guatemala City, Guatemala	Bandar Seri Begawan, Brunei
Kuwait, Kuwait	Ljubljana, Slovenia
Luxembourg, Luxembourg	Mbabane, Swaziland
Mexico City, Mexico	Ouagadougou, Burkina Faso
Panama City, Panama	Sri Jayawardenapura Kotte, Sri Lanka
Singapore, Singapore	Yamoussoukro, Côte d'Ivoire

A Run for the Border

The borders where countries meet are some of the most interesting places on Earth. The longest border in the world is the Canada–U.S. border, more than five thousand miles long, and it's still largely undefended. Even though Canada is the second-biggest nation on Earth, the United States is its only land neighbor.

Sixteen other countries in the world have only one neighbor (Brunei, Denmark, Dominican Republic, Gambia, Haiti, Ireland, Lesotho, Monaco, Papua New Guinea, Portugal, Qatar, San Marino, South Korea,

Timor-Leste, United Kingdom, and Vatican City). How many can you find on a map, Junior Geniuses?

By contrast, Russia and China hold the record for *most* neighbors. They touch fourteen other nations each—including each other.

Mr. Russia's Neighborhood	Mr. China's Neighborhood
Azerbaijan	Afghanistan
Belarus	Bhutan
China	India
Estonia	Kazakhstan
Finland	Kyrgyzstan
Georgia	Laos
Kazakhstan	Mongolia
Latvia	Myanmar
Lithuania	Nepal
Mongolia	North Korea
North Korea	Pakistan
Norway	Russia
Poland	Tajikistan
Ukraine	Vietnam

There are forty-five countries—that's more than 11 percent of the Earth—that are landlocked, meaning they don't touch the ocean. As you can imagine, this makes international trade, to say nothing of beach vacations, difficult. The biggest landlocked nation is Kazakhstan, at over a million square miles. It does border the Caspian Sea, which (as we learned) is actually a big lake.

What if a country is landlocked *and* every country it borders is also landlocked? These nations are said to be "doubly landlocked," and there are only two in the world right now: tiny Liechtenstein, sandwiched between Austria and Switzerland, and Uzbekistan, in Central Asia.

Junior Genius Joviality

Teacher: Johnny, can you tell me where Uzbekistan is?

Johnny: I sure can't, teacher.

Teacher (*annoyed*): Go stand in the corner, young man.

Johnny: Okay. (*He does.*) I still don't see it.

BONUS TIP: Bet someone that, no matter what city or country they name, you can tell a joke about it. Then just tell the above joke, replacing Uzbekistan with their suggestion!

Small World

I assume most of you Junior Geniuses are from a very large country—the United States, for example, or

(where applicable) Canada. But let me introduce you to the world's five *smallest* countries, the ones you need a magnifying glass to find on a map.

VATICAN CITY

> **AREA:** 0.17 square miles, smaller than a golf course
> **SO SMALL THAT:** It doesn't have a single street sign!

MONACO

> **AREA:** 0.78 square miles, smaller than New York's Central Park
> **SO SMALL THAT:** Its national orchestra is bigger than its army!

NAURU

> **AREA:** 8.2 square miles, the size of Disneyland Paris
> **SO SMALL THAT:** Only two countries (Australia and Taiwan) maintain embassies there!

TUVALU

> **AREA:** 9.9 square miles, smaller than JFK Airport
> **SO SMALL THAT:** It paid for its first paved streets and streetlights by selling the rights to its Internet domain, ".tv"—but, ironically, the country doesn't even *have* broadcast TV!

SAN MARINO

> **AREA:** 61 square miles, smaller than Washington, D.C.
> **SO SMALL THAT:** It's possible for tourists to take a snapshot of the entire country!

Pop Quiz!

What nation is only 109 miles wide, on average, even though it's twenty-five times that long from north to south?

Of course, small countries can be big in other ways. The nation of Singapore is so small you can drive across it in half an hour, but the little island is home to more than 5 million people, making it the second most densely populated nation on Earth. (Monaco is in first place. The lowest population density? Mongolia. With only four people per square mile, you don't have to worry about running into your neighbors too often.)

Kiribati is only 313 square miles in area, but because its islands span the equator *and* the 180th meridian, it's the only country in the world that covers all four hemispheres: the Northern, Southern, Eastern, and Western!

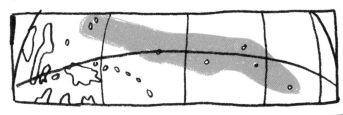

Extra Credit

Saudi Arabia is one of the world's biggest countries (the twelfth biggest, larger than Mexico) but, amazingly, it doesn't have *a single permanent lake or river!* The country relies on wells, seasonal rainfall, and desalinated seawater to quench its thirst.

That's Our Name (Don't Wear It Out)

Would you be surprised to know, Junior Geniuses, that Japanese people don't live in Japan, or Finns in Finland? The Japanese name for Japan is actually Nippon. In Finnish, Finland is Suomi.

In fact, there are lots of countries on Earth that we English speakers don't call by their correct names.

Algeria's full name in Arabic is Al-Jumhūriyyah al-Jazā'iriyyah al-Dīmuqrāṭiyyah al-Sha'biyyah, so I guess it probably takes a while to say the Pledge of Allegiance there.

But many countries have full English names that are a real mouthful as well. Lots of countries are just the Republic of this or the Kingdom of that, but

Bolivia is now the Plurinational State of Bolivia. Fancy! ("Plurinational" means diverse or multicultural.) Brunei, a small sultanate on the island of Borneo, is officially the State of Brunei, Abode of Peace. San Marino has been the Most Serene Republic of San Marino since its constitution was adopted in 1600, making it the world's oldest surviving republic!

New Or "New"?

There are lots of countries older than San Marino. Egypt's been around for like six thousand years. But here are the world's *newest* countries, some of which are probably younger than you are!

SOUTH SUDAN. Born in July 2011, when it seceded from Sudan.

KOSOVO. Born in February 2008, when it declared independence from Serbia.

MONTENEGRO. Born in June 2006, when it *also* voted to separate from Serbia.

EAST TIMOR. Born in May 2002, gaining independence from Indonesia.

PALAU. Born in October 1994, from a UN-administered territory in the Pacific.

The Country Formerly Known As . . .

The United States of America has gone by the same name since July 1776, but other places like to switch it up a bit more. Istanbul was Constantinople, as the song goes. Junior Geniuses: Can you match these modern countries with their old-timey names? The Internet or an encyclopedia might help.

Today	Back Then
1. Belize	a. Bechuanaland
2. Benin	b. British Honduras
3. Botswana	c. Ceylon
4. Burkina Faso	d. Dahomey
5. Democratic Republic of the Congo	e. Gold Coast
6. Ghana	f. New Hebrides
7. Iran	g. Persia
8. Sri Lanka	h. Siam
9. Thailand	i. Upper Volta
10. Vanuatu	j. Zaire

ANSWERS:

1. ⬠, 2. ⬡, 3. ◺, 4. ◹, 5. ◺, 6. ☐,
7. ◣, 8. ◮, 9. ⬡, 10. ☐

Pole Position

For more than thirty years, the North African country of Libya had one of the world's most distinctive flags by having the *least* distinctive flag: just a plain green rectangle! The civil war that overthrew Libya's longtime president Muammar al-Qaddafi in 2011 also got rid of the all-green flag.

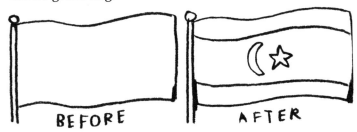

BEFORE   AFTER

So the world's most unusual flag might now be Nepal's.

NEPAL   SWITZERLAND   VATICAN CITY

It's not even a rectangle—it's shaped like two overlapping triangular pennants! (Two countries, Switzerland and Vatican City, currently have flags that are squares.)

There's also the Paraguayan flag.

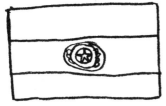

FRONT

Nothing odd there, right? Well, walk around the flagpole and look again.

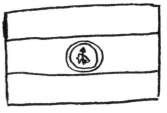

BACK

That's right—Paraguay is the only country in the world whose flag looks different on the back.

Extra Credit

The flag of Papua New Guinea, a stylish design featuring the Southern Cross and a bird of paradise, was actually designed in 1971 by Susan Karike, a fifteen-year-old schoolgirl who won a nationwide contest!

MUSIC CLASS

When you think about it, "The Star-Spangled Banner" is a pretty weird choice for America's national anthem. It's hard to sing, nobody knows the words, and it commemo-rates a random naval battle of the War of 1812. But plenty of other countries have strange anthems as well.

Many have lyrics that are even more warlike than America's. In Vietnam, for example, they sing, "Our glorious path is built on the corpses of our foes." France's famous anthem, "La Marseillaise," sounds inspiring, but the first verse is pretty gross, warning of "ferocious soldiers" coming "to cut the throats of your sons and women"! The goriest anthem has to be Algeria's—because it was originally written in blood! Its composer used his own blood to scratch it on his prison cell walls when the French army took him captive in 1956.

If you're going to mention a different nation in your anthem, Spain is a popular choice. The first verse of the Dutch national anthem, weirdly, still declares allegiance to the king of Spain! (Spain ruled the Netherlands in 1574, when the words were written.) Argentina's anthem, though, calls the Spanish "fiery tyrants" and

"vile invaders." (Those verses don't get sung much anymore.) One anthem that *doesn't* mention Spain belongs to . . . Spain itself! Their anthem is just instrumental: It has no lyrics at all.

The people of Liechtenstein were just as lazy. They wrote lyrics for their anthem but borrowed their music from Britain's national anthem, "God Save the King," which causes much confusion whenever the two countries meet at soccer matches.

Some anthems have more distinguished pedigrees. Japan's is a poem dating back over a thousand years. Norway and Bangladesh commissioned words from Nobel Prize–winning authors. Mozart is credited with the melody of Austria's anthem, and Haydn wrote Germany's. The anthem of Barbados was written by Lord Burgess, a calypso musician most famous for writing Harry Belafonte's version of "The Banana Boat Song" (a.k.a. that song where they say "Day-O!"). Burgess wasn't even *from* Barbados! He just happened to be visiting the island one time and got asked to pitch in with the anthem.

But other national anthem composers don't get no respect. George Kakoma had to sue the government of Uganda to get them to admit that he'd written their anthem. In the end, they paid up: two thousand Ugandan shillings, about seventy-eight cents.

Greece has the longest national anthem—the poem they use as their song has 158 stanzas, so the whole thing would take almost an hour to sing!

SIXTH PERIOD

Cities and Landmarks

We may think of cities as a modern invention, Junior Geniuses, but in fact human beings have been crowding together for survival for almost ten thousand years. Archaeologists digging around the Middle East have found villages there that were inhabited going back to the Stone Age, some with thousands of residents. Maybe one of them is Bedrock, where the Flintstones used to live.

These ancient settlements didn't have freeways and parking meters and Starbucks, but they were cities all the same. Damascus, for example, the capital of Syria, has probably been continuously inhabited for more than nine thousand years! I live in a city that was founded the same year as the passenger elevator. Damascenes live in a city that's much, much older than the wheel!

Even the first metropolises, or super-cities, are sur-

prisingly old. Around the time of its first emperor, Augustus Caesar, Rome had more than a million people, making it the first city ever to have a population top seven digits. And these hip urbanites had many of the conveniences of modern life: indoor plumbing, central heating, concrete buildings, and an empire crisscrossed by 180,000 miles of paved roads—more than three times the length of the U.S. interstate system today! Rome's Circus Maximus, where chariot races were held, could hold 150,000 spectators. That's the capacity of Candlestick Park and Cowboys Stadium *combined*.

The City That Never Sleeps

They even had traffic jams in the ancient world! Julius Caesar got so fed up with rush hour in Rome that he banned all wheeled vehicles from the city's street during daylight hours. Unfortunately, this just led to lots of noisy nighttime cart traffic . . . and lots of annoyed Romans. "Insomnia is the main cause of death in Rome," complained the poet Juvenal at the time.

Other cities would continue to hit the seven-figure mark in the centuries to come, including Alexandria, Baghdad, and Beijing. At the time the Spanish conqueror Hernán Cortés invaded Mexico in 1519, the Aztec capital of Tenochtitlán was a clean, beautifully designed city of canals, gardens, markets, and pyramids, bigger than London and Paris put together! "Some of our soldiers asked whether or not it was all a dream," one Spaniard wrote in his journal.

Big City Life

Today Tenochtitlán is called Mexico City, and it's grown a *lot*, with 21 million people in its metropolitan area. *¡Es muy grande!* But it's not the world's most populous city, not by a long shot. Here's the history of the "World's Biggest City" title since the Aztec Empire's heyday:

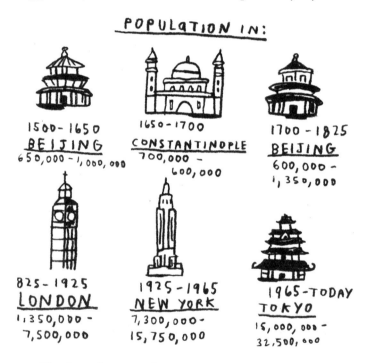

POPULATION IN:

1500-1650
BEIJING
650,000 - 1,000,000

1650-1700
CONSTANTINOPLE
700,000 - 600,000

1700-1825
BEIJING
600,000 - 1,350,000

825-1925
LONDON
1,350,000 - 7,500,000

1925-1965
NEW YORK
7,300,000 - 15,750,000

1965-TODAY
TOKYO
15,000,000 - 32,500,000

That's right: Population-wise, Tokyo has been the capital of the world since 1965, when men still wore hats and hamburgers cost a quarter.

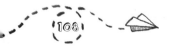

If anything, that whopping 32.5 million number is misleadingly *low*, since it was Tokyo's urban population in Japan's 2000 census. If we use the United Nations' latest population estimates for cities (they call them urban agglomerations, which is fun to say) then there are actually 37 million people or so in the Tokyo region. So it's way ahead of runners-up Seoul, Mexico City, and New York.

Thirty-seven million! To put that into perspective:

○ That's about the same size as the population of California! (Only imagine those people crammed into an area smaller than Connecticut.)

○ Tokyo's Shinjuku Station is the busiest train station in the world, handling 3.64 million passengers *every day*. That's roughly the population of Panama—the entire country!—passing through one of its two hundred–plus entrances every twenty-four hours.

WEEE!

∘ Streets in Tokyo are so crowded that residents aren't even allowed to buy a car unless they get a *shako-shomei* certificate, proving that they already have a parking space for it.

∘ The city has more than fifteen hundred McDonald's restaurants, almost twice as many as the great state of Texas.

∘ The Tokyo area does about $2 *trillion* worth of business every year. So if Tokyo were an independent country, it would be the ninth-biggest economy on the planet, bigger than that of India, Canada, or Russia.

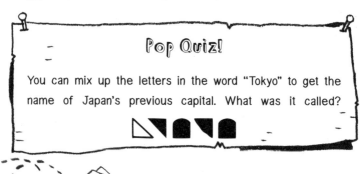

Pop Quiz!

You can mix up the letters in the word "Tokyo" to get the name of Japan's previous capital. What was it called?

Urban Sprawl

When we talk about the world's largest cities, we usually mean the largest population. But what about area? What are the world's biggest cities *geographically*?

It turns out that the world's most sprawling cities don't look much like cities at all. For example, take the state of Alaska. Because so much of Alaska is sparsely populated, cities and boroughs (which are the Alaskan equivalents of counties) don't have separate governments. The city limits are the same as the county border. This means that a "city" like Yakutat—really an isolated town of 691 people on the shores of an icy, glacier-surrounded bay—is technically six times the size of Rhode Island!

The other big cities all use the same loophole. The city of Kalgoorlie-Boulder, in Australia, really should put the word "city" in quotation marks. It's a vast desert wasteland surrounding two small towns . . . and yet it's run by a mayor and city council. Altamira, in the jungles of northern Brazil, is even bigger, a "city" that's about the size of the state of Illinois.

The world champ is Hulunbuir, in the remote Chinese grasslands of Inner Mongolia. This sparsely populated region is more than 100,000 square miles in area, bigger

than the United Kingdom. But China administers it as a "prefecture-level city," so a city it is! (Even if it's a "city" with more shepherds than shoppers and more camels than cabs.)

Call Me That Maybe

People who travel a lot often note that Greenland is icy, but Iceland is fairly green. Shouldn't their names be the other way around? Greenland's name dates back to around AD 982, when the Norse explorer Erik the Red was exiled from his home in Norway. He sailed to a new northern island, which he named Greenland as a marketing ploy, hoping to get settlers to move there with him.

Erik knew that the names of places can be powerful things. This explains why St. Paul, the capital of Minnesota, is no longer called Pig's Eye Landing, like it was when it was first founded. (It was named for its founder, a fur trader and bootlegger named Pierre "Pig's Eye" Parrant, who sounds like a pretty cool guy.)

Save the Wales

But sometimes an awkward name can put a town on the map. Take the Welsh village of Llanfair Pwllgwyngyll. That's already enough of a tongue twister to me, but in the 1860s, a local tailor decided the town could bring in more tourists if its name was *even longer*. So he led a successful campaign to rename the city (deep breath): Llanfairpwllgwyngyllgogerychwyrndrobwllllantysiliogogogoch.

In Welsh, this fifty-eight-letter mouthful of a name means "Mary's church in the hollow of the white hazel near the rapid whirlpool and the church of St. Tysilio with a red cave."

It worked! More than two hundred thousand visitors still come every year to admire the twenty-foot railroad sign with the town's preposterously long name.

Extra Credit

Llanfairpwllgwyn-whatever isn't the *world's* longest-named city, however. That honor belongs to the city of Bangkok, Thailand. You see, only foreigners call the city Bangkok. Locals call it Krungthep, which is short for (even deeper breath):

Krungthepmahanakhon Amonrattanakosin Mahintharayutthaya Mahadilokphop Noppharatratchathaniburirom Udomratchaniwetmahasathan Amonphimanawatansathit Sakkathattiyawitsanukamprasit.

The translation for Krungthep is "city of angels." Get a stopwatch and see how quickly you can say the full Thai name. If you can get under thirty seconds, I'll be impressed.

Here are a few oddly named towns that probably have a lot of trouble with sign theft.

Okay, this ski town actually has two dots over the *E*. (It's pronounced "POO-kuh," from the Latin *via publica*, meaning "public road.") But the city's welcome sign doesn't have two dots, so it's still a target for giggling tourists.

This yawner of a Portland suburb bills itself as "The Most Exciting Place to Live."

In 2008, the mayor of Batman threatened to sue Warner Bros. for using its town name in the *Dark Knight* movies without permission. Holy nuisance prosecution, Batman!

This town almost changed its name to Lost Farm after having to replace its sign four times in five years. In the end, they settled for welding the new sign to its pole and embedding it in concrete.

This Bavarian town isn't as stinky as it sounds. The name probably comes from *rotte* and *Ecke*—German for "red corner."

Local Yokels

You'd think it would be easy to tell someone's hometown from its adjective form. A New Yorker is from New York; a Roman is from Rome. But where's a Porteño from, or a Mancunian? If you ever meet one of these mystery men and women, just consult this handy chart:

a (an)...	is from...
Angeleno	Los Angeles, California
Cairene	Cairo, Egypt
Capetonian	Cape Town, South Africa
Capitalino	Mexico City, Mexico
Caraquenian	Caracas, Venezuela
Carioca	Rio de Janeiro, Brazil
Glaswegian	Glasgow, Scotland
Haligonian	Halifax, Canada
Madrileño	Madrid, Spain
Mancunian	Manchester, England
Münchner	Munich, Germany
Muscovite	Moscow, Russia
Neapolitan	Naples, Italy
Porteño	Buenos Aires, Argentina
Varsovian	Warsaw, Poland

Pop Quiz!

What word can be used for an ancient Mediterranean civilization or a resident of the capital of Arizona?

Tall Tales

Earthquakes and fires long ago wiped out six of the Seven Wonders of the Ancient World. Only the Great Pyramid of Giza is still standing.

In fact, in the year AD 1300, almost four thousand years after it was built, the Great Pyramid was still the tallest human structure on Earth. But from that point on, things escalated pretty quickly.

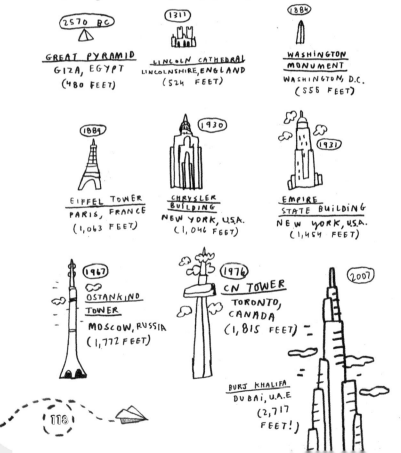

2570 BC
GREAT PYRAMID
GIZA, EGYPT
(480 FEET)

1311
LINCOLN CATHEDRAL
LINCOLNSHIRE, ENGLAND
(524 FEET)

1884
WASHINGTON
MONUMENT
WASHINGTON, D.C.
(555 FEET)

1889
EIFFEL TOWER
PARIS, FRANCE
(1,063 FEET)

1930
CHRYSLER
BUILDING
NEW YORK, U.S.A.
(1,046 FEET)

1931
EMPIRE
STATE BUILDING
NEW YORK, U.S.A.
(1,454 FEET)

1967
OSTANKINO
TOWER
MOSCOW, RUSSIA
(1,772 FEET)

1976
CN TOWER
TORONTO,
CANADA
(1,815 FEET)

2007
BURJ KHALIFA
DUBAI, U.A.E
(2,717 FEET!)

When the Burj Khalifa was completed in 2007, it was six times taller than the Great Pyramid, which was the last Middle Eastern building to hold the title of tallest structure. But no pyramid could have all the fancy stuff that the Burj does: 206 stories, elevators that travel at forty miles per hour, the world's largest shopping mall, and a man-made lake underneath.

Extra Credit

The world's largest *office building*, however, is the Pentagon outside Washington, D.C., headquarters of the U.S. Department of Defense. With twenty-five thousand workers spending the day there, the Pentagon is really a miniature city, including twenty restaurants, a gym, a chapel, a nail salon, an art gallery, and even a Best Buy. The whole thing covers six separate ZIP codes!

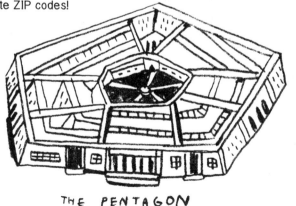

THE PENTAGON

Local Color

The Burj Khalifa's 24,438 windows require a small army of window washers, working for three or four months, to get them all clean. It's a glass surface the size of twenty-two football fields, after all! But at least the building doesn't have to be *painted*. Just in case you ever want to paint your room to match the Golden Gate Bridge or the Eiffel Tower, here are the paint colors used for some of the world's most famous landmarks:

○ INTERNATIONAL ORANGE. The Golden Gate Bridge isn't golden at all, but rather this shade of orange vermilion paint. Thirteen ironworkers and twenty-eight painters walk the seven-hundred-foot-high cables of the bridge year-round, replacing rivets and touching up paint.

∘ **LONDON FOG.** There's been some controversy at New York's famous Guggenheim Museum lately over what color its exterior should be. Architect Frank Lloyd Wright originally chose a pale yellow for the building, but for the last couple of decades, it's been this shade of light gray instead.

∘ **WHISPER WHITE.** This Duron shade is currently used for the White House in Washington, D.C. When the exterior was restored in 1992, workers removed *thirty-two layers* of white paint that had been slapped on over the years!

∘ **GALAXY GOLD.** When Seattle's Space Needle opened in 1962, the top saucer was this bright orange, with highlights of Orbital Olive, Re-Entry Red, and Astronaut White. The roof was repainted white for many years, but Galaxy Gold was brought back in 2012 for its fiftieth anniversary.

○ EIFFEL TOWER BROWN #1–3. Paris's famous tower has had many shades of brown over the years, but the current batch of paint is a rich bronze color. Or should I say colors? There are actually three shades of paint getting progressively lighter as you go up the tower. Why? Tower officials say that it's "to complement the color of the Paris sky."

Eiffel Sour

Many Parisians actually hated the Eiffel Tower at first. Hundreds of famous artists and writers signed a petition opposing its construction. Writer Guy de Maupassant famously ate lunch every day in the restaurant at its base—because, he said, that was the only place in Paris where he could avoid seeing the tower! But the once-hated tower is now Paris's most enduring symbol—and the world's most visited monument (if you don't count free ones).

Bird's-Eye Views

It's often said that the Great Wall of China is the only human structure visible from space, or from the moon. Junior Geniuses, *this is not true.*

The Great Wall of China *is* an amazing feat, of course: thirteen thousand miles of wall, made up of almost 4 billion bricks mortared together with rice flour. But there are two problems with seeing it from space:

1. It's too narrow.

2. It's the same color as the ground around it.

Even from low Earth orbit, China's first astronaut said he couldn't find the wall—but lots of other human structures are easily visible, including airports, bridges, and dams.

123

Here are four pieces of art that can *only* be enjoyed from high above the Earth:

○ **THE NAZCA LINES.** The world's biggest graffiti are these ancient geoglyphs carved into the desert of southern Peru. There are dozens of drawings, including hummingbirds, monkeys, spiders, and condors.

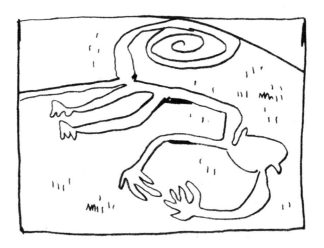

○ **THE WORLD, DUBAI.** Sheikh Mohammed of the United Arab Emirates created three hundred sandy islands in the Persian Gulf in the shape of the continents, hoping celebrities would buy miniature versions of their favorite destinations. Then the real estate market collapsed and the islands started to sink.

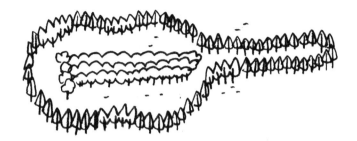

∘ **THE FOREST GUITAR.** On the Pampas of Argentina, a rancher planted more than seven thousand trees into the shape of a guitar over two-thirds of a mile long. His young wife, a musician, had always planned to plant a guitar-shaped field, but died before she could fulfill her dream. The guitar is his tribute to her.

∘ **SPIRAL JETTY.** In 1970, artist Robert Smithson used a fleet of dump trucks to bring 6,550 tons of dirt and rock to the Great Salt Lake in Utah, where he arranged them into this fifteen-hundred-foot spiral. Unfortunately, his giant sculpture was built during a historic drought, and it's been mostly underwater since then.

Pop Quiz!

What city is home to the famous Pont Neuf over the Seine River? The name means "new bridge," even though it's the city's *oldest* bridge.

Statue Secrets

The world's three tallest statues are all carvings of the Buddha, recently completed in Asia. The tallest, China's Spring Temple Buddha, is half the height of the Chrysler Building, so tall that the Statue of Liberty would look like a hobbit standing next to it.

Junior Geniuses, can you keep a secret? Here are five EXTREMELY CONFIDENTIAL FACTS about the world's famous statues:

1. THE GREAT SPHINX OF GIZA WAS A CARTOON SUPERVILLAIN! There are still traces of red, yellow, and blue paint on the surface of the sphinx, suggesting that it was once painted in bright primary colors. Archaeologists have also found remains of two accessories it used to wear: a pointy beard and a big cobra headdress. Yes, the Sphinx looks awesome today, but you should have seen it four thousand years ago!

2. THERE'S A HIDDEN VAULT INSIDE MOUNT RUSHMORE! Gutzon Borglum, who carved the presidents on Mount Rushmore, wanted the mountain to contain a hall of records, with America's most important documents stored inside. In 1998, Borglum's dream came true, and

sixteen carved panels were sealed in a titanium vault under a half-ton piece of granite. The capsule is supposed to stay buried for thousands of years—but you'd never see it anyway. The hall of records is off limits to visitors.

3. THE EASTER ISLAND HEADS AREN'T JUST HEADS! The island's famous *moai* statues are usually referred to as "heads," but actually all the sculptures have full bodies buried in the rich volcanic soil. A few even have legs.

4. THE LITTLE MERMAID KEEPS GETTING DISMEMBERED! This bronze version of the Hans Christian Andersen fairy-tale character is the most famous symbol of Copenhagen, Denmark—but not everyone's a fan. In 1964, a revolutionary art group sawed off her head and stole it, and her right arm was stolen in 1984. The replacement head was stolen *again* in 1998—but quickly returned and reattached. Hmm, maybe she should have stayed "under the sea."

GRRRR

5. THE STATUE OF LIBERTY ALMOST FEATURED A LAXATIVE AD! Everyone knows that Lady Liberty was a gift from France, but only Junior Geniuses know that we almost didn't want it. The statue was supposed to be a centennial gift in 1876 but fund-raising efforts to build a pedestal for the statue ground to a halt, so the statue stayed in France for years. Finally, newspaperman Joseph Pulitzer took up the cause, promising to print the name of everyone who donated to the pedestal fund. Money started pouring in, and the makers of Castoria laxative offered to pitch in $25,000 if the pedestal included a big ad for their bowel-loosening product. Luckily, their offer was declined.

Potty All the Time

Like Copenhagen and New York, Brussels, Belgium, also has a statue as its most iconic landmark . . . but this statue is a little different. Manneken-Pis ("Little Man Pee") is a naked little bronze boy caught in the act of, well, peeing into a fountain. He's based on a legend about a two-year-old prince who peed on some enemy Flemish soldiers in the twelfth century.

SEVENTH PERIOD

The Fifty States

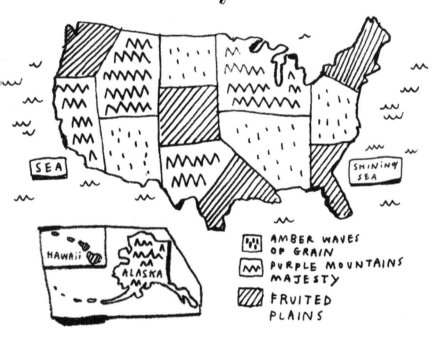

SEA

SHINING SEA

HAWAII

ALASKA

AMBER WAVES OF GRAIN

PURPLE MOUNTAINS MAJESTY

FRUITED PLAINS

Junior Geniuses, this is the United States of America.

Like most of us, the United States has gotten bigger—a lot bigger—as it's grown up. If you were a schoolchild in 1790—and I hope you weren't, because if so that means you've flunked over two hundred times—American geography was much easier. There were a lot fewer state capitals to learn.

1790

Number of states: 13

Population: 3,929,214 (about the size of Los Angeles today)

Land area: 864,746 square miles (about the size of Saudi Arabia today)

Hobbies: Whittling, eating johnnycake, powdered wigs

Bonus Junior Genius Math Lesson!

You can compute a place's population density with one easy equation:

$$\text{POPULATION DENSITY} = \frac{\text{POPULATION}}{\text{AREA}_{sq.mi}}$$

So in 1790, America's population density was . . .

$$3,929,214 \ / \ 864,746 = 4.54.$$

So that's just 4.5 people living in every *square mile* of the country. Today that would make it the least densely populated country on Earth, even lonelier than Iceland or Mongolia!

Over the next century, the familiar outline of the United States gradually formed on maps, a patchwork of land added via treaty and transaction.

This new territory gradually got added in the form of states, so the flag got more crowded.

Star Treatment

Originally, when new states were added to the Union, the American flag got a new star *and* a new stripe! The flag that Francis Scott Key saw waving over Baltimore in 1814, the one that inspired him to write "The Star-Spangled Banner"? Well, Vermont and Kentucky had recently been granted statehood, so the flag that night had actually had fifteen stars *and fifteen stripes*!

Luckily, in 1818, lawmakers realized that their plan was going to make the flag awfully crowded eventually, so they decided to hold the number of stripes to thirteen, in honor of the original colonies, forever. Good thing, too, or today's American flag would look like this:

(WE COULDN'T EVEN FIT IN ALL THOSE STARS AND STRIPES!)

And the map grew as well.

1840

Number of states: **26**

Population: **17,069,453** (about the size of Cairo, Egypt, today)

Land area: **1,749,462 square miles** (about the size of India and Pakistan today)

Hobbies: **Sod houses, shooting "varmints," typhoid**

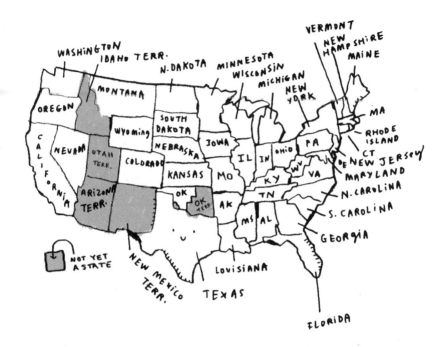

1890

Number of states: **44**

Population: **62,947,714** (about the size of the United Kingdom today)

Land area: **3,540,705 square miles**

Hobbies: **Barbershop music, bicycles with one big wheel and one small wheel, mustache wax**

1940

Number of states: **48**

Population: **132,164,569** (about the size of Japan today)

Land area: **3,554,608** square miles

Hobbies: **Jitterbugging, comic books, stickball**

Finally, in 1959, America bought a little corner box
to keep Alaska and Hawaii on, creating the map we still
know today.

Today

Number of states: **50**

Population: **314,712,000**

Land area: **3,537,438 square miles**

Hobbies: **Fast food, hipsters, Facebook** (the hipsters are not on Facebook)

Setting the Record State

Today's fifty states range from the largest (Alaska) to the smallest (Rhode Island), from the sunniest (Arizona) to the flattest (Florida) to the most pizza-eating (New Hampshire) to the nerdiest (Ohio; 6.9 library visits per Ohioan per year).

Even though Rhode Island is the smallest state, it does at least have the longest name! It's officially the State of Rhode Island and Providence Plantations.

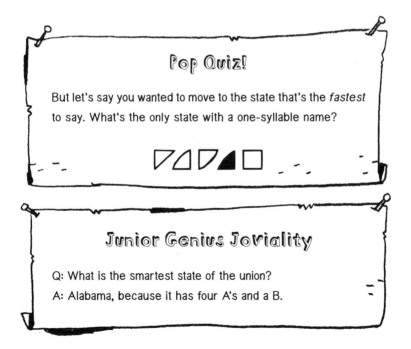

Pop Quiz!

But let's say you wanted to move to the state that's the *fastest* to say. What's the only state with a one-syllable name?

Junior Genius Joviality

Q: What is the smartest state of the union?
A: Alabama, because it has four A's and a B.

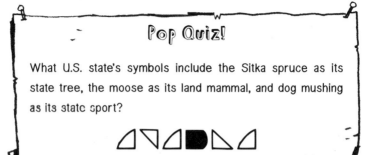

Pop Quiz!

What U.S. state's symbols include the Sitka spruce as its state tree, the moose as its land mammal, and dog mushing as its state sport?

But My Friends Call Me ...

Most state nicknames are pretty easy to understand. There was a gold rush in the Golden State (California). The Peach State (Georgia) grows the most peaches. Arizona is the Grand Canyon State because it has, duh, a really big canyon.

But what's a "Hawkeye" or a "Hoosier"? Indian tribes? Kinds of bird, maybe? This handy guide will help you decipher the seven oddest, old-timiest state nicknames.

THE BUCKEYE STATE

From the buckeye tree, whose nuts resemble the eye of a deer. "Buckeye" was the nickname of a few early Ohio settlers, including future president William Henry Harrison, and the name stuck.

Coined back in the 1780s, possibly by George Washington himself. New York was the nation's capital, the "Seat of the Empire," until 1790.

Probably for the Sauk Indian chief Black Hawk, who died in Iowa.

"Hoosier" has meant "country bumpkin" since the 1820s—but nobody knows why! It might come from the British term "hoozer," or the New Orleans slang "husher." A famous Indiana poet joked that there were so many barroom brawls in his state that "Hoosier" originally meant "Whose ear?"—like, "Hey, whose ear is this on the floor?"

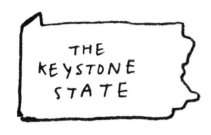

If the thirteen original U.S. colonies formed an arch, then Pennsylvania—the big, important one in the middle—was their keystone.

Named for the Maryland Line, a Revolutionary War regiment that made a heroic stand at the 1776 Battle of Long Island.

From Missouri's nineteenth-century reputation for skepticism and straight talk. Popularized by a congressman who said, in 1899, "Frothy eloquence neither convinces nor satisfies me. I'm from Missouri, and you have got to show me!"

Cross-Country

As you can probably guess from looking at a map, Alaska is both the northernmost and westernmost state of the union. The northernmost point is a peninsula just north of Barrow, an Alaskan town so far north that polar bears roam the outskirts of town and night lasts a full month during the winter. If you're looking for warmer waters, head to the lava cliffs of Ka Lae, at the southern tip of the island of Hawaii, where you'll find the nation's southernmost point.

What about America's easternmost point? Would you guess Maine? Or Florida? Think again, Junior Geniuses. The easternmost point of the United States is actually in . . . Alaska! As you can see on this map,

Alaska's Aleutian Islands cross the 180th meridian that separates the two hemispheres. This means that more than a dozen of the Aleutians are actually in the Eastern Hemisphere. So the easternmost point of the United States is an uninhabited volcanic island called Semisopochnoi . . . and it's just sixty-five miles *west* of America's westernmost point, another uninhabited island called Amatignak!

What about the middle of the country? In 1918, a U.S. government surveying office decided to calculate America's exact center using superscientific means: They cut a map of the United States out of cardboard and balanced it on the head of a pin!

The cutout balanced just north of a little town called Lebanon, Kansas. There visitors will find a stone marker and a small wedding chapel there, in case you want to get married *in-the-exact-mathematical-middle-sort-of* of America.

(Actually, the addition of Alaska and Hawaii in 1959 means that America's center is now somewhat farther north, near Belle Fourche, South Dakota. But that town doesn't have as nice a monument!)

Over the Edge

When you drive between states on a highway, all you see is a nice sign welcoming you to Iowa or Texas or someplace. But on a map, you can see that state borders are sometimes a lot more complicated.

FOUR CORNERS. For example, would you say Colorado and Wyoming are perfect rectangles? They *seem* to be. When Congress created those states, they were supposed to be. But nineteenth-century surveying technology didn't have lasers and GPS and so forth, so the borders aren't perfectly straight lines.

As a result, Four Corners Monument, the spot where Arizona, Colorado, New Mexico, and Utah meet, is in the wrong place! The actual place where the states were *supposed* to meet is 1,807 feet farther east. That's almost a third of a mile away! (The real spot looks almost the same: same desert, but no souvenir stands.)

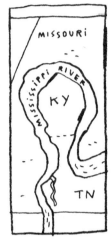

THE KENTUCKY BEND. The surveyors drawing the line between Kentucky and Tennessee weren't 100 percent sure where their border would meet the Mississippi River. When they got there, they realized that a loop in the river had created a tiny island of Kentucky surrounded on all sides by Missouri and Tennessee! Locals sometimes call it Bubbleland.

TWELVE-MILE CIRCLE. The top of Delaware is the only round border in the United States—but it's not a perfect circle. The original land grant that created Delaware defined its border as a twelve-mile radius around the town of New Castle, but it's been surveyed many different times, so the circle is a little wobbly. (Today, the New Castle courthouse dome is used as the center.)

ELLIS ISLAND. New York and New Jersey have long argued over who owns this famous gateway of American immigration. Originally, the island was part of New

York, but the river was New Jersey's. But as New York expanded the island in the early twentieth century, New Jersey complained that the new parts of the island were coming out of the river, and should therefore be part of New Jersey! Finally, in 1998, the Supreme Court ruled that New Jersey does indeed own most of Ellis Island.

Extra Credit

Missouri and Tennessee border the most other states with eight neighbors each, including each other. Maine is more of an introvert: It borders only one other state. Hawaii, of course, has no neighbors. But, oddly, it does have interstate highways!

Hometown, U.S.A.

America's highways can take you anywhere from Aaronsburg, Pennsylvania, to Zzyzx, California. (Zzyzx, pronounced "ZYE-zix," is a dry lake bed in the Mojave Desert of California where a con man named Curtis Howe Springer built a phony mineral spa in 1944. According to the U.S. Board on Geographic Names, it's alphabetically the last place in America.)

My own grandfather came from Muleshoe, Texas, so I've always been a fan of the weirdest place-names from small-town America. Here's one from each state of the union.

Burnt Corn, Alabama

Deadhorse, Alaska

Why, Arizona

Turkey Scratch, Arkansas

You Bet, California

Hygiene, Colorado

Puddle Town, Connecticut

Shortly, Delaware

Yeehaw Junction, Florida

Hopeulikit, Georgia

Volcano, Hawaii

Good Grief, Idaho

Normal, Illinois

Santa Claus, Indiana

Diagonal, Iowa

Swamp Angel, Kansas

Monkey's Eyebrow, Kentucky

Wham, Louisiana

Suckerville, Maine

Accident, Maryland

Satans Kingdom, Massachusetts

Nirvana, Michigan

Nimrod, Minnesota

Whynot, Mississippi

Frankenstein, Missouri

Zero, Montana

Gross, Nebraska

Roach, Nevada

Cowbell Corners, New Hampshire

Buttzville, New Jersey

Pie Town, New Mexico

Handsome Eddy, New York

Boogertown, North Carolina

Porcupine, North Dakota

Fort Fizzle, Ohio

Pumpkin Center, Oklahoma

Drain, Oregon

Pillow, Pennsylvania

Woonsocket, Rhode Island

Ketchuptown, South Carolina

Red Shirt, South Dakota

Bugtussle, Tennessee

Ding Dong, Texas

Eggnog, Utah

Mosquitoville, Vermont

Lick Skillet, Virginia

George, Washington

Looneyville, West Virginia

Embarrass, Wisconsin

Chugwater, Wyoming

Selling Out

Some American towns have figured out that they can boost tourism or even cash fat corporate checks by changing their names. Here are my five favorites:

1. TRUTH OR CONSEQUENCES, NEW MEXICO. In 1950, a popular radio quiz show called *Truth or Consequences* announced that they would broadcast their program from the first city to rename itself after the show. Hot Springs, New Mexico, was tired of being confused with other cities called Hot Springs and happily made the change.

2. JIM THORPE, PENNSYLVANIA. Legendary athlete Jim Thorpe never visited the former Mauch Chunk, Pennsylvania, but the town bought his remains in 1953, hoping that visiting sports fans would keep the town afloat when the coal mines there closed down.

3. HALF.COM, OREGON. The town of Halfway, Oregon, agreed to name itself after the shopping website Half.com at the height of the Internet boom in 1999. It was a happy ending for everyone. The sleepy Oregon town got $110,000 and twenty computers for its local school district, while Half.com got purchased by eBay for $300 million.

4. JOE, MONTANA. In 1993, the town of Ismay, Montana, population twenty-two, changed its name temporarily to Joe, in a publicity stunt dreamed up by the Kansas City Chiefs to honor quarterback Joe Montana.

5. TOPIKACHU, KANSAS. In August 1998, the capital of Kansas, Topeka, celebrated the debut of the first Pokémon game by renaming itself Topikachu for the day. In 2010, the city renamed itself Google for the month, hoping that Google would install a new fiber-optic network there for free. It didn't.

All right, class. We've learned a lot today—are you ready to officially certify as a Junior Genius Maps and Geography expert? Remember: Don't get too stressed about this test. Just relax and do your best, because these results will stay on your permanent record **forever**. Get out your sharpened number 2 pencils and turn the page when I say "Begin."

Wait for it.

Wait for it . . .

BEGIN.

1. Thimphu, Bhutan, is the only world capital without a single what?

 Ⓐ fire station   Ⓑ traffic signal

 Ⓒ McDonald's   Ⓓ airport

2. During the seventeenth century, what mistake did Europeans make on their maps of California?

 Ⓐ leaving it off   Ⓑ drawing it three times too large

 Ⓒ putting it in South America   Ⓓ making it an island

3. What happens at the mid-ocean ridge?

 Ⓐ the seafloor spreads apart   Ⓑ islands are born

 Ⓒ the ocean becomes saltier   Ⓓ Aquaman tapes his TV courtroom show

4. What was the first city in human history to reach a population of one million inhabitants?

 Ⓐ Rome   Ⓑ Tokyo

 Ⓒ London   Ⓓ Kolkata

5. Which of these holidays happens while it's winter in Australia?

 Ⓐ Easter   Ⓑ Christmas

 Ⓒ Halloween   Ⓓ the Fourth of July

6. Shinjuku, in Tokyo, is by far the world's busiest what?

Ⓐ seaport   Ⓑ train station

Ⓒ stock exchange   Ⓓ karaoke bar

7. What is Challenger Deep?

Ⓐ the deepest part of the ocean floor   Ⓑ a Russian borehole project

Ⓒ the Pacific's farthest spot from land   Ⓓ the sea under the Arctic ice cap

8. What has disastrously happened to the Aral Sea in the last fifty years?

Ⓐ it's flooded   Ⓑ it's become polluted

Ⓒ it's become a war zone   Ⓓ it's shrunk

9. Brazil's capital city, Brasilia, was designed to look like what on a map?

Ⓐ a star   Ⓑ an airplane

Ⓒ a parrot   Ⓓ a soccer ball

10. Which of these imaginary lines is drawn to pass through Greenwich, England?

Ⓐ the prime meridian   Ⓑ the international date line

Ⓒ the Tropic of Cancer   Ⓓ the equator

11. Alphabetically, what's the first of the four U.S. states that meet at Four Corners Monument?

Ⓐ Arizona   Ⓑ Arkansas

Ⓒ California   Ⓓ Colorado

12. The world's sixty tallest volcanoes are all in what mountain range?

Ⓐ the Himalayas   Ⓑ the Rockies

Ⓒ the Andes   Ⓓ the Alps

13. In what state would you find Semisopochnoi Island, technically America's easternmost point?

Ⓐ Maine   Ⓑ Florida

Ⓒ Alaska   Ⓓ Hawaii

14. Until recently, what country's flag was just a solid green rectangle?

Ⓐ Mozambique   Ⓑ Pakistan

Ⓒ Venezuela   Ⓓ Libya

15. What fifth ocean was officially added to maps in 2000?

Ⓐ the African   Ⓑ the Southern

Ⓒ the Greenland   Ⓓ the Occidental

16. What makes the town of Lebanon, Kansas, geographically special?

Ⓐ It's the hottest place in the U.S.

Ⓑ It has only one resident

Ⓒ It's the center of the contiguous United States

Ⓓ It exists only on maps

17. What is the Earth's largest desert?

Ⓐ the Sahara

Ⓑ the Gobi

Ⓒ the Antarctic

Ⓓ the Arabian

18. Where would you find the structure that was Earth's tallest for thousands of years?

Ⓐ Britain

Ⓑ China

Ⓒ India

Ⓓ Egypt

19. What is the oldest surviving globe called?

Ⓐ continent ball

Ⓑ parlor planet

Ⓒ earth apple

Ⓓ spinny map

20. The Ring of Fire is the zone where you'd find 90 percent of the world's what?

Ⓐ rain forests

Ⓑ earthquakes

Ⓒ diamonds

Ⓓ coral

All right, pencils down! Turn the page to the answers and see how you did.

ANSWERS

1.	2.	3.	4.	5.
6.	7.	8.	9.	10.
11.	12.	13.	14.	15.
16.	17.	18.	19.	20.

Scoring

16–20	Certified Junior Genius!
13–15	In the Neighborhood
10–12	Just Offshore
6–9	The Farside of the World
0–5	You Just Guessed B for All of Them, Didn't You?

Did you make the cut, Junior Genius? If so, go to JuniorGeniusGuides.com to print out your certificate! I'm proud of you.

If you didn't quite pass, don't worry! Take another look at the book to review, and try the test again. You get as many tries as you need. Remember: Being a Junior Genius is about curiosity and perseverance, not grades.

(But you also need a good grade.)

HOMEWORK

If today's lesson has left your mappetite unsatisfied, there are lots of ways to explore geography outside of class. Here are some ideas:

○ BECOME A CARTOGRAPHER. Try to draw a map of your school or neighborhood from memory. Have friends or family members do the same, and compare your maps. Did everyone remember the same landmarks, or are the maps very different? Now compare your map to a digital one, and see how close everyone came. Are there things that *everyone* drew wrong?

○ TRAVEL BACK IN TIME. The Internet makes it easy to find old maps. If you live in a U.S. city, you might like the amazing collection of beautiful, old panoramic maps that the Library of Congress keeps at memory.loc.gov/ammem/pmhtml. See how your city looked a century ago or more. Did your neighborhood even exist, or was it just forest or prairie back then?

◦ **TAKE A ROAD TRIP.** The next time you're in the car for a longish drive, appoint yourself the navigator. If you have a GPS device, shut it down and use a paper map or road atlas instead, just like people used to in the olden days (the 1990s). Can you find the shortest route to your destination? Are there any cool side trips you want to recommend to the driver? Can you figure out how to predict how many miles you're traveling, or the kind of terrain you'll be passing through?

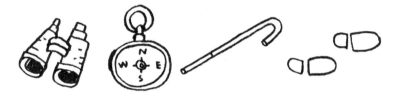

◦ **DISCOVER HIDDEN TREASURE.** Have a grown-up take you "geocaching." On geocaching.com, you'll be able to find a list of your nearest caches—hidden containers that can be located with a GPS device. The ones highlighted in light green are beginner caches, and most likely, there will be several within walking distance of where you live! Bring a pen and maybe a small toy, since some geocaches have room for little trinkets you can swap.

THE FINAL BELL

Do you know the story of . . .

∘ The man with one hundred eyes who still managed to fall asleep on the job, so all his eyes got taken away and put on a peacock tail?

∘ The baby god who invented the lyre, taught himself to play it, and stole fifty cows by making them wear shoes—all when he was just one day old?

∘ The giant bronze man who ran around the island of Crete once a day, wrecking pirate ships by throwing boulders at them?

Our next class together will be **Ken Jennings' Junior Genius Guides: Greek Mythology.** Make sure you're in your seats when the bell rings. I'll see you then.

Until we meet again, remember the official Junior Genius slogan. In the words of the great French thinker Blaise Pascal: "It is much better to know something about everything than everything about something."

Class dismissed!